Capital Structure and Firm Performance

In the complex world of finance, understanding the relationship between a company's capital structure and its overall performance is crucial. This book offers a comprehensive exploration of the interdependence between capital structure decisions and business performance, with a specific focus on German-listed companies. It provides valuable insights into the intricate dynamics of corporate finance.

Through a blend of theoretical frameworks, empirical research, and practical applications, the book presents readers with a thorough understanding of how capital structure decisions impact a company's profitability, risk profile, and long-term sustainability. From traditional theories of capital structure to cutting-edge empirical methodologies, the book outlines the latest developments in the field, offering practical tools and strategies for optimising financial decision-making. Moreover, the book explores how different regions and global trends influence capital structure decisions, providing a comprehensive examination of varying practices and the factors that shape them. It delves into specific aspects influencing global capital structures, including an analytical comparison of capital structures across key global markets such as the United States, the European Union, and China. This comparison highlights how economic, cultural, and market dynamics influence corporate leverage decisions. The impact of technological innovations and their role in reshaping financial strategies are also discussed.

Designed for scholars, researchers, and advanced students in finance and economics, this book serves as a definitive reference for understanding the complex dynamics of corporate finance. With its rigorous analysis and practical insights, it equips readers with the knowledge and analytical tools needed to navigate the challenges of capital structure decision-making in today's dynamic business environment.

Ewelina Sokołowska is Professor of Economics and Finance and Head of the Department of Digital Economy and Finance, Faculty of Management and Economics, Gdańsk University of Technology, Poland.

Milad Zargartalebi is Lecturer of Economics and Finance in the Faculty of Business Administration, Nuremberg Institute of Technology Georg Simon Ohm, Germany.

Routledge Focus on Economics and Finance

The fields of economics are constantly expanding and evolving. This growth presents challenges for readers trying to keep up with the latest important insights. Routledge Focus on Economics and Finance presents short books on the latest big topics, linking in with the most cutting-edge economics research.

Individually, each title in the series provides coverage of a key academic topic, whilst collectively the series forms a comprehensive collection across the whole spectrum of economics.

The Chief Financial Officer and Corporate Performance
Finance, Governance and Risk
Elżbieta Bukalska, Anna Wawryszuk-Misztal and Tomasz Sosnowski

Artists Labour Market, Cultural Policy and Creative Economy
A Triangular Model in Poland
Dorota Ilczuk, Anna Karpińska, Emilia Cholewicka

Reading John Maynard Keynes
A Short Introduction
Andrés Solimano

Regional Economic Integration in East Asia
Institutions, Agreements and the European Experience
Magdalena Suska

Capital Structure and Firm Performance
Global Financing Decisions among Listed Companies
Ewelina Sokołowska and Milad Zargartalebi

For more information about this series, please visit: www.routledge.com/Routledge-Focus-on-Economics-and-Finance/book-series/RFEF

Capital Structure and Firm Performance

Global Financing Decisions among Listed Companies

Ewelina Sokołowska and Milad Zargartalebi

Routledge
Taylor & Francis Group
LONDON AND NEW YORK

First published 2025
by Routledge
4 Park Square, Milton Park, Abingdon, Oxon OX14 4RN

and by Routledge
605 Third Avenue, New York, NY 10158

Routledge is an imprint of the Taylor & Francis Group, an informa business

British Library Cataloguing-in-Publication Data
A catalogue record for this book is available from the British Library

Library of Congress Cataloging-in-Publication Data
Names: Sokołowska, Ewelina, author. | Zargartalebi, Milad, author.
Title: Capital structure and firm performance : global financing decisions among listed companies / Ewelina Sokołowska and Milad Zargartalebi.
Description: Abingdon, Oxon ; New York, NY : Routledge, 2025. | Series: Routledge focus on economics and finance | Includes bibliographical references and index.
Identifiers: LCCN 2024040936 (print) | LCCN 2024040937 (ebook) | ISBN 9781032898988 (hardback) | ISBN 9781032899008 (paperback) | ISBN 9781003545194 (ebook)
Subjects: LCSH: Corporations—Finance. | Capital. | Organizational effectiveness.
Classification: LCC HG4026 .S634 2025 (print) | LCC HG4026 (ebook) | DDC 658.15—dc23/eng/20241029
LC record available at https://lccn.loc.gov/2024040936
LC ebook record available at https://lccn.loc.gov/2024040937

ISBN: 978-1-032-89898-8 (hbk)
ISBN: 978-1-032-89900-8 (pbk)
ISBN: 978-1-003-54519-4 (ebk)

DOI: 10.4324/9781003545194

Typeset in Galliard
by Apex CoVantage, LLC

Contents

Tables

Figures

Abbreviations

ANN	Artificial neural network
AT	Asset turnover
CAP	CAPEX/total assets
CEO	Chief executive officer
DE	Debt equity ratio
EBIT	Earnings before interest and taxes
EI	EBIT/interest expense ratio
GAAP	Generally accepted accounting principles
GW	Generalised weights
IFRS	International Financial Reporting Standards
IPO	Initial public offering
LTD	Long-term debt divided by total assets
OM	Operating margin
PB	Price-to-book ratio
PE	Price-to-earnings ratio
PPE	Property, plant, and equipment
PRO	Year-on-year profit growth
R&D	Research and development
RBV	Resource-based view
REV	Year-on-year revenue growth
ROA	Return on assets
ROE	Return on equity
ROIC	Return on invested capital
SME	Small- or medium-sized firm
TOL	Tolerance
VIF	Variance inflation factor
YoY	Year on year

Introduction

It is essential, in today's business landscape, to have a deep understanding of capital structure and its effects on a company's performance. The capital structure is the combination of debt and equity that a company uses to fund its operational and strategic decisions. Companies have two main financing options: internal and external financing. Internal financing utilises resources like cash flow and retained earnings, while external financing entails raising funds through bank loans, corporate bonds, or equity offerings. The decision between these options can have a substantial impact on a company's financial stability and the strategic possibilities of the enterprise.

According to various concepts, such as the Modigliani-Miller theorem, under certain conditions, a firm's value is unaffected by its capital structure. However, real-world complexities like taxes, bankruptcy fees, and asymmetric information raise many doubts about this idea. Despite extensive study efforts, our understanding of the factors that influence capital structure remains insufficient. It also highlights substantial differences between different businesses and industries. This underscores the importance of conducting additional research, especially concerning the impact of a company's performance on its financing decisions.

Several theoretical models provide suggestions for capital structure decisions. For instance, the trade-off theory suggests that firms balance the tax benefits of debt against the costs of potential financial distress. The pecking order hypothesis argues that corporations prioritise internal finance, followed by debt, and ultimately equity, based on the idea of least effort and asymmetric information. Furthermore, the agency theory investigates conflicts of interest between management and shareholders, emphasising debt's role in reducing agency costs. Empirical research has shown conflicting conclusions on the ideal capital structure. According to certain research, a larger leverage ratio can help firms operate better. Some studies indicate that a higher leverage ratio can improve firm performance by providing tax shields and enforcing managerial discipline. Conversely, other research highlights the risks associated with high leverage, such as

DOI: 10.4324/9781003545194-1

increased bankruptcy probability and agency costs. This ambiguity necessitates a deeper investigation into the factors that drive capital structure decisions and their impact on performance.

To measure the performance of a company's operations, we often use financial indicators. They include profit margin, return on assets (ROA), and return on equity (ROE). These metrics enable a critical assessment of the company, most often over time, allowing analysis of its efficiency, effectiveness, and competitive position in the industry. They not only evaluate financial results but also consider broader aspects of value creation and sustainable development. As a result, the concept of a company's performance is multifaceted and includes various dimensions such as operational efficiency, market share, and innovative capacity. Traditional performance measures focus on financial results, but modern approaches also include non-financial metrics. They also include customer satisfaction, employee involvement, and social responsibility. This holistic approach recognises that sustainable performance requires balancing financial success with the company's long-term strategic goals.

Research has focused on the link between capital structure and firm performance, with varying degrees of success. Some studies suggest that a higher debt ratio can enhance performance through tax benefits and managerial discipline, while others point out the risks of financial distress and agency costs associated with high leverage. Moreover, there is increasing interest in reverse causality, which also concentrates on the idea that firm performance influences capital structure decisions. Understanding this relationship requires examining various factors, including firm size, industry characteristics, and macroeconomic conditions. For example, small firms may face higher costs of external financing due to information asymmetry and limited collateral. In contrast, large firms can access diverse financing sources and negotiate better terms. Industry dynamics also play a crucial role, as capital-intensive industries may rely more on debt to finance significant fixed assets, whereas technology firms might prefer equity to support innovation and growth.

Empirical research that looks into the causes and effects of capital structure only produces mixed results when it comes to the logic of financing choices. This means that there is a "gap in our understanding of what determines heterogeneity in capital structure" (Lemmon et al., 2008). A large meta-analysis that looks at 90 primary empirical studies and 266 models (Schneider, 2010) says that we still don't know for sure what the main capital structure determinants do (Schneider, 2010). The author also asserts that Modigliani and Miller's (1958) famous irrelevance theorem continues to significantly influence research on capital structure determinants.

Furthermore, empirical research "shows that a large amount of variation [among the capital structure among companies] remains unexplained after controlling for firm-level characteristics" (Bertrand & Schoar, 2003).

As a result, optimising a firm's capital structure is still relevant in academic research. Hence, especially when considering unique conditions, questions on what determines the capital structure do still remain (Brusov et al., 2022). Given these results, it is tempting to evaluate the role of performance in capital structure research. We can mention this topic as a field with ambiguous results (Eriotis et al., 2002; Kebewar, 2013; Ramachandra & Nageswara Rao, 2008), so it is worth further exploration.

A closer examination of the relationship between capital structure and performance is necessary, given the relatively broad concept of performance and the similarities between the concepts of firm performance and business performance. Financial theory typically assumes that the structure of capital influences the performance of a specific firm. We typically address this relationship by focusing on the leverage ratio, which is the key ratio of the capital structure, and its role in explaining firm performance (e.g., Chen, 2004; González, 2013).

The main goal of this monograph is to fill this gap by investigating these relationships in a broad range of industries, focusing on publicly listed German companies. The existing literature primarily addresses the direct impact of capital structure on performance, often neglecting the potential reverse relationship. While some studies investigate this reverse causality, they typically confine their scope to specific sectors, such as banking, thereby limiting the generalisability of their findings. Additionally, the influence of macroeconomic factors and institutional frameworks on capital structure decisions and performance outcomes remains underexplored. To address these gaps, this monograph adopts a comprehensive approach, considering a wide array of variables and employing robust methodologies. The study benefits from a homogeneous regulatory and economic environment because it focuses on German firms, allowing for a more precise analysis. However, the findings may also provide insights applicable to other contexts, given the global nature of financial markets and corporate strategies. The research adopts an exploratory approach to address the complexities of capital structure and performance relationships. Utilising financial data from publicly listed German companies ensures a homogeneous context for analysis. The methodology includes various forms of regression analysis and artificial neural network (ANN) analysis to uncover direct and recursive relationships between the studied variables. The use of regression analysis allows for identifying significant predictors of capital structure and performance, while ANN analysis provides a more nuanced understanding of complex, non-linear relationships. This dual-method approach enhances the robustness and validity of the findings, offering a comprehensive view of the relationship between capital structure and firm performance.

The monograph has the following structure: The first chapter introduces theories and literature about capital structure. It starts by introducing the concept and theories of capital structure, discussing traditional theories such as trade-off theory and pecking order theory. The chapter then explores newer perspectives and empirical research on capital structure decisions by firms. It provides a comprehensive overview of the major theories, their implications, and the empirical evidence supporting them.

The second chapter focuses on theories and literature related to business performance and firm growth. It begins with an introduction to business performance theories, examining the microeconomic foundations of firm growth and different growth models. The chapter then reviews empirical research on business performance, including studies on general firm performance, change management, turnaround strategies, and performance metrics. It provides insights into the factors that influence business performance, as well as the approaches used to measure and analyse them.

Chapter three concentrates on global perspectives on capital structure decisions in various economies. This chapter explores how different regions and global trends influence capital structure decisions, providing a comprehensive examination of varying practices and the factors that shape them. Each section aims to focus on specific aspects of global capital structures. The first section provides an analytical comparison of capital structures across key global markets, including the United States, the European Union, and China. It discusses how economic, cultural, and market dynamics influence corporate leverage decisions. Then, the focus shifts to how technological innovations, particularly fintech and blockchain, are reshaping financial strategies. The section examines the direct impact of these technologies on capital raising, debt management, and equity distribution. It also explores how technology offers new opportunities and challenges in maintaining an optimal capital structure. The next part addresses the complex landscape of global and regional regulations that affect capital structure decisions. In this section, the discussion is about how compliance affects strategic financial planning and the adaptation strategies businesses employ to align with these regulatory frameworks. Then, the chapter explores how different capital structures can mitigate or amplify the risks associated with business operations. Finally, this section delves into how sustainability and environmental, social, and governance (ESG) criteria are increasingly influencing capital structure decisions. It covers the growing trend of green bonds, sustainable financing, and how companies integrate ESG factors into their financial strategies to attract ethical investments and ensure long-term profitability. This part will also highlight global trends and showcase companies that have successfully integrated ESG into their capital structures.

Chapter four outlines the study's research design. It covers various aspects such as research philosophy, data model, research questions, hypotheses, sampling, data collection methods, and an overview of variables. The chapter also discusses the data analysis procedures and methods employed in the study, including bivariate analysis, regression analysis, group comparison analysis, and artificial neural network analysis.

The last chapter presents the empirical analysis conducted as part of the study. It begins with descriptive statistics to summarise the data, followed by bivariate analysis to examine relationships between variables. We applied regression analysis, group comparison analysis, and artificial neural network analysis to examine the inverse relationship between capital structure and business performance. We evaluate and discuss the results, taking into account the limitations of the analysis.

The monograph concludes by summarising the study's key findings and drawing conclusions based on empirical analysis. We presented the findings' implications for theory and practice. The chapter also reflects on the limitations of the study and suggests directions for future research in the field. Overall, it provides a comprehensive synthesis of the research conducted in the book. Apart from the main chapters, the book includes additional components such as references, a list of tables and figures, abbreviations, and appendices containing supplementary information or data analysis. These components contribute to the completeness and professionalism of the book.

This monograph contributes to the academic discourse on capital structure and business performance by providing new insights into their reciprocal relationship. It emphasises the importance of understanding how different financial strategies impact firm success. It also offers practical recommendations for managers to optimise their capital structure for better performance. Additionally, the methodological innovations, particularly the use of ANN analysis, represent a valuable contribution to the research toolkit in this field. The study's theoretical contributions include refining existing models of capital structure and performance by incorporating recursive relationships and contextual factors. This approach challenges traditional assumptions and provides a more holistic understanding of financial decision-making. Practically, the findings offer actionable insights for managers and policymakers, highlighting the importance of aligning capital structure strategies with performance objectives and external conditions. By addressing these complex relationships, the monograph advances theoretical knowledge and provides actionable insights for practitioners, enhancing their ability to make informed financial decisions that drive long-term success. It underscores the relevance of strategic financial management to achieving sustainable growth and competitive advantage.

In conclusion, this monograph aims to bridge the gap between theory and practice in the study of capital structure and firm performance, offering a comprehensive analysis that is both academically rigorous and practically applicable. Through detailed empirical research and innovative methodologies, it seeks to enhance our understanding of these critical business dynamics, ultimately contributing to more effective and strategic financial decision-making. The study's significance extends beyond academic and managerial circles, providing valuable implications for investors, regulators, and other stakeholders. By elucidating the factors that drive capital structure decisions and their impact on performance, the monograph contributes to more transparent and efficient financial markets. Furthermore, it highlights the need for continuous adaptation and innovation in financial strategies, ensuring that firms remain resilient and competitive in an ever-changing business environment.

1 Capital Structure Theories – A Deciphering Tool for Successful Businesses

1.1 Understanding the Essence of Capital Structure

The task of determining how different types of capital finance a firm's assets is known as capital structure. Capital can take various forms, such as debt, equity, or hybrid securities issued by the firm (Myers, 1984). Corporate finance research includes decisions that impact companies' capital structures. These are practically relevant for financial managers within firms (Renzetti, 2001). Empirically, choices that refer to the capital structure, like the question of how much debt a firm should issue, are different across various companies. Despite years of research on this theme in financial academic theory (Brusov et al., 2022; Modigliani & Miller, 1958), many findings and decisions concerning capital structure are still relevant and, to some degree, unexplained. The literature also refers to capital structure as a type of indicator that measures the source, composition, and proportion of a firm's debt and equity capital. Therefore, the design of the capital structure impacts various business and governance domains such as the operating environment, the rights and obligations of shareholders, the decision-making bodies, changes in the governance structure, and the future development of a firm (Luo & Jiang, 2022).

The extensive research on capital structure in academic financial research has resulted in a variety of approaches to this topic. This context necessitates the mention of distinct schools of thought or views on the topic. These include, for example, the notion of whether the capital structure is relevant or irrelevant to performance (Ogebe et al., 2013). Generally, we can classify the variety of different approaches to capital structure theories available in the academic literature into two categories: a traditional approach and a modern view. The traditional approach focuses on the operational activity of the firm. The traditional approach views financing solely as a necessary tool in the production process of goods. We assume that the real economic process and the business process and its requirements are the primary factors influencing

DOI: 10.4324/9781003545194-2

capital needs, financing procedures and, ultimately, the capital structure (Ogebe et al., 2013; Renzetti, 2001). On the other hand, the modern view considers the unique conditions that arise within the context of individuals associated with companies, as well as their specific interests and incentives. These include, for example, the firm's owners and management, who pursue the maximisation of the company's value or their own interests and consciously make financing decisions. Here, issues of asymmetric information and agency problems are present (e.g., Akerlof, 1970; Jensen & Meckling, 1976; Ross, 1977). These approaches strongly link investment and financing decisions, or capital structure decisions, to the goal of satisfying the demands of stakeholders outside the firm (Simerly & Li, 2000). In principle, we can classify approaches to explaining the capital structure of firms into two different schools of thought. These include the neoclassical theories of corporate finance, as well as the neo-institutionalist financing theory. Capital structure theories provide approaches to determining the extent to which and under what circumstances a stock market listing or the company's ownership structure can influence financing decisions.

According to the neoclassical financing theories' assumptions, these two factors should not affect the capital structure. Neo-institutionalist theories say that decisions about capital structure may be different in family businesses versus non-family businesses, publicly traded companies versus privately traded companies, because shareholders and (external) managers may not have the same amount of information or may have principal-agent conflicts (Jensen & Meckling, 1976; Ross, 1977). We will delve deeper into the modern approach's theories in the subsequent sections. So, let's take a deeper look at the neoclassical approach that exists in the literature. The neoclassical theory is based on firm management's central tenet, which is to maximise the firm's value to shareholders, claiming that capital markets are efficient. Within the neoclassical approach, individuals act rationally and without behavioural biases regarding their decision-making (Vasiliou & Daskalakis, 2009). The efficient capital markets theory, also known as the efficient market hypothesis, has its roots in Fama's work (1970). Neoclassical theories are also relevant in capital structure research, although they have macroeconomic applications. Gordon (1992) noted that the neoclassical theory of investment has a significant influence in this context. The application of neoclassical thinking in capital structure research began in the 1960s, with its theoretical underpinnings based on the assumption that capital markets are complete and efficient, thereby assuming rational decision-making and behaviour by individuals such as investors, shareholders, and managers. A key example of this is the irrelevance proposition theorem of Modigliani and Miller (1958; Tirole, 2005). The trade-off theory is another approach to explaining capital structure in the neoclassical realm. Here, the focus is on finding the best mix of debt and equity in order to reduce overall financing costs to an optimal level (Fama & French, 2002).

In contrast to neoclassical theories, neo-institutionalist financing theories do not assume information-efficient markets. The neo-institutionalist financing theories' approaches extend the neoclassical approaches by making significant assumptions. They are based on the assumptions that (1) information asymmetries exist between the individual actors and (2) principals and agents pursue specific objectives and make decisions based on an individual utility function (Ross, 1977). Thus, the neo-institutional corporate finance theory largely refers to the principal-agent theory (Jensen & Meckling, 1976).

The new institutional economics, which began in the 1970s, focused on corporate governance issues. Researchers in this field have questioned the role of information asymmetries, as well as the impact of associated transaction and agency costs. Neo-institutionalist finance theories argue that the acquisition of information is not (always) possible without costs, or that information asymmetries exist and cause these costs for the actors (Akerlof, 1970; Myers & Majluf, 1984). For example, external investors cannot fully assess the value of a company or the skills of a manager. Furthermore, the theory strand considers the heterogeneity of managers' interests in contrast to those of the firm's shareholders or other capital providers (Jensen & Meckling, 1976; Ross, 1977). In neo-institutionalist models, information asymmetries and potential principal-agent costs can influence corporate policy decisions, such as capital structure. As a result, capital structure decisions must also consider principal-agent conflicts of interest (Tirole, 2005). Theoretically, we can distinguish the neo-institutional approaches into two categories: agency theory, which addresses the mentioned conflicts of interest, and signal theory, which addresses communication issues to resolve agency conflicts (Vernimmen, 2018, preface p. IX). However, we will only mention these distinctions here and not assign them a key role further below.

Researchers have developed behavioural approaches based on the empirical finding that financial behaviour and capital structure decisions have deviated from the neoclassical paradigm. Behavioural finance attempts to explain certain phenomena by decoding the behaviour of financial managers and applying it to capital structure theories. The literature (Vasiliou & Daskalakis, 2009) claims that these generally yield better results.

We must distinguish the behavioural approaches from the principal-agent theory, even though they both highlight the significance of behaviour. However, whereas the principal-agent theory is concerned with behaviour as a result of asymmetric information and its respective results (e.g., Jensen & Meckling, 1976), behavioural approaches have a much broader scope. Studies such as Bertrand and Schoar (2003) and

Graham and Harvey (1997) highlight various areas where managers' personal interests or personality traits influence capital structure decisions.

1.2 Major Theories Shaping Financial Strategy

The first part evaluated and grouped the capital structure literature according to its various approaches. The various strands offer structure and direction to the overall field of academic research on this subject, emphasising several unique aspects. While this provides an overview, it is not sufficient for understanding capital structure theory, as it is a necessity in shaping the firm's financial strategy. Therefore, we will mention and discuss the primary theories in capital structure research to delve deeper into this crucial topic.

In the traditional approach to capital structure research, the capital structure matters due to differences in the cost of debt and equity. In the event of bankruptcy, debt holders have a superior claim over equity holders on the remaining firm value, meeting their claims before the firm's owners. According to this understanding, as debt levels rise, the weighted average cost of capital (WACC) decreases, reaching a point where debt levels are no longer sustainable (Brusov et al., 2022). Modigliani and Miller (1958) then criticised the traditional approach's relevance to the capital structure, asserting in their famous irrelevance theorem that the capital structure was irrelevant. Because the capital structure is irrelevant, corporate financing should have no impact on firm value or capital costs. The result is based on the following assumptions (Brusov et al., 2022; Modigliani & Miller, 1958):

1. No tax payments;
2. The existence of a perfect market with a symmetric information distribution implies the absence of information asymmetries.
3. There are no transaction costs within an atomistic market structure.
4. No bankruptcy costs;
5. Equal borrowing costs apply to both the company and investors.

Assuming that the capital structure has no effect on the value of the company in efficient markets, the capital structure as a result of financial policy should be irrelevant for capital structure decisions concerning the use of the different financial instruments and the leverage level (Modigliani & Miller, 1958). Moreover, the capital costs are independent of the debt level. Consequently, financing decisions are independent from investment decisions in an efficient and complete market. Only real activities, such as investments capable of increasing net income, can create value, not dividend policies or other financing methods (Tirole, 2005). We can state the result of the irrelevance theorem as the reason listed companies should not have an advantage over private companies, meaning the ownership structure has no bearing on the firm's financial decisions.

Modigliani and Miller (1958) also note that leverage increases lead to a decrease in capital costs required that the company dispose of sufficient profitable investment options compared to the opportunity cost of not using such profitable business opportunities due to avoiding debt financing. The optimal debt-to-equity ratio (leverage) is the point of maximum corporate value. However, in the case of positive bankruptcy costs, the debt ratio increase also results in increasing bankruptcy risks, leading to a higher risk premium for debt capital providers and, thus, to higher capital costs for the company (Wohlenberg & Plagge, 2012).

The original model by Modigliani and Miller did not consider bankruptcy costs, and the absence of taxes can also be considered a critical factor. However, in a later article, the authors discussed the effect of taxes on their model, resulting in an extension of the original model by the incorporation of taxes as a relevant factor or a capital-structure determinant (Modigliani & Miller, 1963). The main reason for considering the role of taxes is the existence of tax shields as a result of the leverage level. By incorporating the beneficial tax treatment of using debt to finance a company, it is not possible to derive an optimal capital structure anymore (Brusov et al., 2022).

Further research on this issue has pointed to another problem of using leverage: Rising leverage increases the insolvency risk, so that risk costs must also be included, as these costs limit the debt ratio and, thus, affect the capital structure (Altman, 1984; Kraus & Litzenberger, 1973; Scott, 1977; Stiglitz, 1969). By extending the original Modigliani-Miller model by considering bankruptcy risks and the effect of taxation, the so-called trade-off theory of capital structure was developed, which aims at explaining the optimal capital structure by determining the minimum capital costs under the assumption that taxes and bankruptcy risks are present (Brusov et al., 2022; Vernimmen, 2018). The fundamentals of the trade-off theory are explained below.

According to the trade-off theory, companies choose the optimal capital structure (debt-to-equity ratio) that minimises capital costs while increasing the risk of bankruptcy associated with higher debt levels. Furthermore, the model explaining capital structure management must include the decision-relevant effects of corporate taxes on debt capital and equity capital. Specifically, the tax advantages of the deductibility of interest payments need to be considered in this context (Fama & French, 2002), similar to the extension of the original irrelevance theorem (Modigliani & Miller, 1963). The trade-off theory exists in two versions: the static trade-off theory and the dynamic trade-off theory (Brusov et al., 2022). Below, we provide a more detailed explanation:

1. *Static trade-off theory:* This version of the trade-off theory applies to a single-period context, where a low leverage level hints at the benefits

of using the tax advantages of debt financing. This leads to a lower WAAC and a generally growing capitalisation for the firm. However, with increasing bankruptcy risk, the costs of financial distress are considered with increasing intensity (Brennan & Schwartz, 1978; Brusov et al., 2022; Leland, 1994).

2. *Dynamic trade-off theory:* Here, additional factors are taken into account that have no influence on single-period decisions but are relevant in decisions concerning multiple periods for capital structure adjustments. This includes, for example, the expectations about future investment and financing opportunities, as well as the transaction costs associated with them (Strebulaev, 2007). Financial decisions in the dynamic trade-off theory are therefore largely based on what a firm anticipates (Brennan & Schwartz, 1984).

While the static and dynamic trade-off theories differ with respect to the period that they refer to, it can be stated that the optimal level of debt in the capital structure can be found when the value of the tax shield is equal to the risk of financial distress caused by potential bankruptcy (Brusov et al., 2022, p. 59; Fama & French, 2002). Due to this trade-off between the two main factors of influence, it is convenient to depict the trade-off theory visually. Figure 1.1. illustrates this.

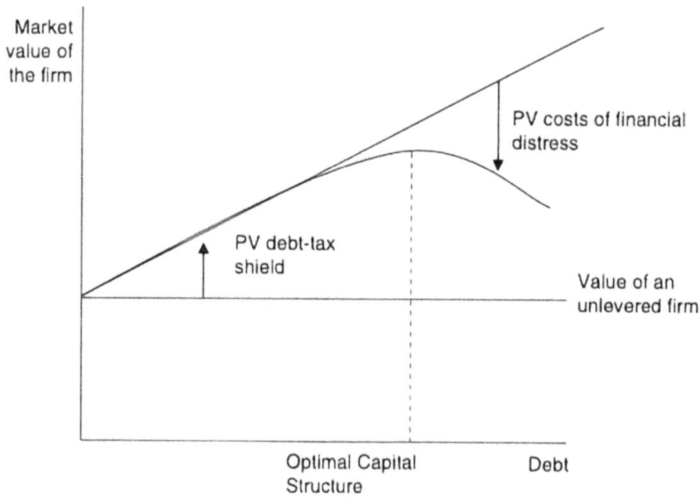

Figure 1.1 Trade-off theory of capital structure

Source: Mac an Bhaird (2010)

Generally, both the irrelevance proposition theorem and the trade-off theory can explain parts of the capital structure puzzle based on differences regarding tax shield benefits, insolvency risk, and transaction costs. However, both theories cannot completely explain why companies are not totally debt-financed. Nevertheless, when considered for the purpose of this thesis, it can be argued that the trade-off theory shows that capital structure determinants clearly impact performance via the impact of interest and tax payments or via the insolvency risk, which, in turn, also relates to the overall business performance of a firm, for example, when a higher insolvency risk leads to a higher overall cost.

Furthermore, recent research rejects the results derived from the perfect market assumptions of the trade-off model. While the basic assumptions for the trade-off theory, assuming an optimal debt-to-equity ratio indicated by an equilibrium, are not considered wrong regarding the benefits of the tax deductibility of interest payments as well as regarding the disadvantages of higher debt capital financing in the form of rising insolvency costs, these are particularly of less relevance. Generally, we must mention other factors that significantly influence financial decisions (Mac & Bhaird, 2010). Furthermore, empirical results indicate that profitable firms are less likely to borrow (Fama & French, 2002; Wald, 1999), raising further questions about capital structure design that the trade-off theory does not address.

Principal-agent relationships also need to be mentioned within the theoretical framework of capital structure theories. These refer to the holders of debt and equity of a firm, where those parties that provide the capital for financing the business are considered principals (debtholders and holders of equity), whereas the firm's management is acting as the agent involved in managing the principal's assets. This relationship leads to a cost, as both the agent and principal are maximising their utility, while the agent does not necessarily act in the best interest of the principal as well. There are three different types of implicit costs involved in the context of principal-agent relationships (Jensen & Meckling, 1976):

1. *Monitoring costs:* costs incurred by the principal, whereby the principal undertakes monitoring in order to ensure that the agent is acting in the interest of the principal for example, by limiting the activities of the agent. For example, a certain level of debt in the capital structure can work as a monitoring mechanism, whereby self-interested managers contain bankruptcy risk (Harris & Raviv, 1991).
2. *Bonding costs:* costs incurred by the agent due to the agent providing credible guarantees for making choices that are going to maximise the utility of the principal. Bonding can take the form of signalling, whereby the agent provides a costly but credible signal to the principal. An example of such a signal is the issuance of debt. By doing so,

firm managers give the signal that they are confident in the firm and in its ability to make timely repayments of the debt (Frydenberg, 2004).

3. *Residual loss:* costs in the form of a loss that is incurred by the principal due to the fact that, despite monitoring and bonding, full alignment of the interests of agent and principal is impossible to perform, so that the agent's activities cannot lead to full maximisation of the welfare of the principal.

Generally, the equilibrium models of the neoclassical approach that integrate taxes and bankruptcy costs assume the existence of an optimal capital structure in which the marginal benefits and marginal costs are balanced out (e.g., Brennan & Schwartz, 1978; Leland, 1994). Based on this fundamental proposition of the existence of an optimal capital structure in a state of equilibrium, the principal-agent theory identifies further advantages and disadvantages of the forms of financing, which are incorporated into the model as benefits or costs (Jensen & Meckling, 1976). Regarding the use of leverage, for example, some of the effects of the principal-agent theory are shown below (Loos, 2006):

- In a company in which managers can maximise their own benefits and make suboptimal decisions for the capital providers accordingly, debt financing can restrict the manager's freedom of decision. A high level of debt reduces the free cash flows available to the management for investment due to the associated interest and repayment obligations. The reduction in free cash flows can, therefore, have a disciplining effect on the managers who maximise the benefits and prevent them from making investments that do not maximise value (Jensen & Meckling, 1976). This means that financing through borrowed capital is accompanied by a benefit for the shareholders, which is all the greater the more pronounced the principal-agent conflicts between managers and owners are.
- Another benefit of debt financing is that managers take on less debt than is necessary to maximise firm value. Such a situation arises when managers are also shareholders, leading to the problem that there is a strong dependence on firm success, so that they tend to be more risk-averse than diversified shareholders. This risk aversion can lead them to avoid the higher insolvency costs associated with debt financing and to refrain from value-maximising investments (Fama, 1980), so that – to the disadvantage of the shareholders – value-maximising investment opportunities may be missed (Finch, 2002). In this case, additional debt capital – and the implementation of value-enhancing investment projects – can lead to an increase in the value of the company and be advantageous for the shareholders.

- However, high-level indebtedness can also result in higher costs and disadvantages, such as the loss of financial flexibility if a company's debt capital capacity decreases. If the debt capital capacity is exhausted, value-increasing investments cannot be made. Thus, the higher the uncertainty about future financing requirements, the more this restriction can lead to costs for the company and its shareholders. Modigliani and Miller (1963) already assumed that, despite tax deductibility, companies do not fully utilise their borrowing capacity but retain a certain flexibility with regard to their financing. Bradley et al. (1984) combine the different views to create a model that considers various costs associated with a high level of debt and weighs these against the tax advantage of debt. Among the costs associated with debt, they combine the factors of the neoclassical models (insolvency costs, taxes) and the principal-agent costs of the neo-institutionalist view.

Other studies have identified significant differences in the capital structure that are often dependent on ownership structure (Volk, 2013). Ownership structure results in differences regarding interests, as well as differences in financing decisions and capital structure, so that privately held high-growth firms generally avoid debt capital (Wu & Au Yeung, 2012).

The neo-institutional theory of the principal-agent problem has already mentioned signalling. Signalling is important in the context of capital structure decisions as a mechanism for mitigating information asymmetries between managers and capital providers (Ross, 1977). Managers have insider information at their disposal, whereas external capital providers do not have equal access to this valuable insider information.

Therefore, outsiders cannot distinguish between different types of companies or whether they are "good" or "bad," similar to the classical lemon problem described by Akerlof (1970). To avoid higher capital costs due to information asymmetries, managers signal to investors that investment projects will increase the company's value. For instance, investors interpret changes in capital structure or dividend payments as a signal for a shift in enterprise value (Masulis, 1983; Miller & Rock, 1985).

As a result, theories involving signalling are highly relevant in capital structure research. This is also relevant in the context of using credit ratings to estimate the effect on the capital structure by applying the leverage-to-profitability ratio as a proxy indicator for both measures. Arnold (2008) finds that if indebtedness increases with decreasing profitability, a credit rating downgrade is likely to occur. Conversely, a company that exhibits a rise in indebtedness in tandem with increasing profitability indicates that the management consistently seeks profitable investment opportunities, utilising both debt and equity capital. This sends a powerful and valuable signal to capital providers, reducing the cost of asymmetric information and, consequently, agency costs. This is likely to finally result in rating improvements for the firm. Otherwise, the finding supports the claim that financing costs grow with increasing levels of asymmetric information.

Myers and Majluf (1984) introduced the pecking order theory, drawing basic assumptions from principal-agent theory. The theory assumes that company insiders have better information than external capital providers, which is a central claim of the principal-agent literature. Information asymmetries lead to adverse selection costs, which influence the financing decision. According to the pecking order theory, enterprises minimise their costs of financing by accounting for the implicit costs of asymmetrical information that accompany the respective financing sources. As a result, firms finance their investments in a particular order. First, firms use retained profits for investments, followed by low-risk outside debt capital. The firm will then use risky external debt capital to finance its projects, with the last option being a fallback to equity under duress and as a last resort (Fama & French, 2002; Myers & Majluf, 1984).

As a result, the pecking order theory provides clear guidance for the selection of different capital sources. This, in turn, has led to criticism of the pecking order theory in the academic literature. Researchers mention that in addition to information asymmetries being central to capital structure decisions, other relevant factors can also cause a pecking order regarding financing instruments. For example, a pronounced control orientation or risk aversion can lead to a focus on internal financing sources. Therefore, many empirical studies (Leary & Roberts, 2010; Myers, 2003) neglect the difficult task of separating the influencing factors.

Furthermore, empirical studies on pecking order theory provide only insufficient and sometimes contradictory results (Leary & Roberts, 2010). In addition, the pecking order theory contradicts the observation that many companies carry out share issues even if they have the possibility to finance themselves with additional debt capital (Fama & French, 2005). Given the existence of different durations of total leverage, the pecking order theory was confirmed by Kuč and Kaličanin (2021) for short-term debt, whereas long-term debt is better explained by referring to the trade-off theory.

Newer financing theories, such as the market timing theory, have emerged in response to the shortcomings of existing capital structure research theories. To illustrate this, we can use the trade-off theory: For listed companies, an increase in the share price changes the ratio of equity to debt capital, whereby the share of equity capital increases. According to the trade-off theory, a company should return to its target capital structure and raise additional debt capital. However, empirical studies show that companies raise equity capital based on market valuation rather than capital structure optimisation concepts at specific times. Companies, in particular, issue shares when investors value them significantly higher than their book values or past market values. Companies also repurchase their own stock in the event of low market values. As a result, firms are generally following market timing logics rather than capital structure optimisation (Baker & Wurgler, 2002).

Baker and Wurgler (2002) argued that these findings are also very persistent. Other studies also confirm the market timing theory's applicability in the context of issuing securities. Implications arise, for example, with respect to IPO pricing in different market situations (Helwege & Liang, 2004; Hoffmann-Burchardi, 2001). The question of whether markets are hot or cold is pertinent not only for equity pricing (Helwege & Liang, 2004) but also for debt financing (Doukas et al., 2011). The majority of company CEOs also state that current market conditions are of major concern when making decisions on capital structure components (Graham & Harvey, 2001). This highlights the key role of market timing in capital structure research.

1.3 Innovative Approaches to Understanding Capital Structure

Having introduced the major theories in the context of capital structure research, it is now worth noting that on the basis of this research, some other more modern approaches have been developed as well. Therefore, at this point, we aim to highlight some of these more recent findings on capital structure research to establish a conclusive foundation for our research on the determinants of capital structure, as detailed in the next paragraph.

Firstly, we should highlight a few selected findings from the field of behavioural finance, a concept we previously introduced in the chapter. The emphasis here is on the crucial role of personality characteristics in managers' decision-making, which also has implications for capital structure research. Below, we mention some selected examples from that research.

Bertrand and Schoar (2003), for example, conclude that the capital structure reflects more the CEO's personal style than the effects of agency costs, tax shields, regulations, or other determinants assumed by mainstream theories. As a result, the authors introduce a human dimension to academic research on capital structure. Financially more aggressive CEOs typically hold less cash but exhibit higher levels of leverage, a strategy ideally employed for firm growth through mergers and acquisitions (M&A). In contrast, more conservative managers typically hold more cash and prefer internal funding for capacity extension financing. However, this results in a lower return on assets compared to aggressive CEOs, except in the case of CEOs with large track records for M&A activities (Bertrand & Schoar, 2003; Graham et al., 2013; Malmendier et al., 2011).

Malmendier et al. (2011) highlight the influence of CEOs' past life experiences on financial policies and the role of overconfidence. Life experiences can include the CEO's experience during times of crisis, which can lead to a greater aversion to risk, such as debt financing. The authors also mention that military experience influences CEOs to select financial policies more aggressively, particularly when it comes to high levels of debt. Generally, overconfidence is a form of bias in decision-making where individuals tend to overestimate the likelihood of their beliefs and actions. There is massive empirical evidence for overconfidence in psychological studies on decision-making (Kahneman & Lovallo, 1993).

Overconfidence can also lead to capital providers engaging in specific actions in order to avoid negative impacts from such behaviour. For example, Voon et al. (2020) demonstrate that bank loan providers adjust loan covenant structures accordingly and tighten access to debt financing in cases of managerial overconfidence.

Psychometric tests have also detected regional differences in managers' psychological traits and attitudes. Research has shown that optimism levels and risk tolerance are different for US managers and non-US managers (Graham et al., 2013). Projects have the potential to enhance the company's value and provide benefits to its shareholders.

Generally, the observations from behavioural studies provide further evidence that more traditional research, like neoclassical or neo-institutional studies on capital structure, provides only a partial view on the topic. It is clear that behavioural factors must also be considered in capital structure research.

Furthermore, some studies point out the existence of market restrictions, particularly those relating to firms' capital supply. However, the lack of specific attention to supply-side restrictions has led to criticism of capital structure theories. Graham and Leary (2011) provide an overview of recent empirical studies on capital structure, which suggests that most theories assume no restrictions on the supply of capital and solely determine the capital structure based on the company's demand for capital. However, companies seeking to raise capital are clearly subject to certain market restrictions and, therefore, cannot raise equity or debt capital indefinitely.

For this reason, some studies examine the limiting factors on the supply side (Faulkender & Petersen, 2006; Leary, 2009; Lemmon & Roberts, 2010; Lemmon & Zender, 2010). For example, information asymmetries at the company level lead investors to restrict the availability of capital. Although a company can take measures to ease financial restrictions, such as applying for a rating, this implementation requires a lot of time and money. On the macroeconomic level, for example, the financial crisis may lead to a reduced supply of capital (Campello et al., 2010).

Putting rules on banks, like Basel II's framework for equity capital, may also have an effect on the supply of debt capital (Kaserer, 2013), which could change how companies can set up their capital structures.

According to the capital structure theory, owners and managers' strategic decisions primarily shape a firm's capital structure (Bromiley, 1991). When a lender determines the amount of financial resources to be allocated to a specific company and its terms, the size of the company or industry can also influence the availability of debt capital (Börner et al., 2010). Therefore, lenders prefer and offer better terms to larger companies in less-risky industries (e.g., the pharma industry) than to smaller companies in riskier industries. Due to the higher likelihood of bankruptcy among SMEs, smaller companies often face limited availability of debt and equity capital (Coleman, 2000; Smolarski & Kut, 2011).

Wu and Au Yeung (2012) found significant and strong negative correlations between high growth and debt issuance among non-financial firms, so that firm performance can explain capital structure heterogeneity. These findings corroborate the findings of Lemmon et al. (2008) and Volk (2013), suggesting that the neoclassical capital structure theory alone cannot explain the determinants of heterogeneity in capital structure. As a result, the evidence suggests that growth plays a significant role in capital structure selection.

In addition, the analysis of the capital structure usually distinguishes only between classical debt and equity and does not address the specific characteristics of the financing instruments. Additionally, the analysis typically does not fully address subcategories or mixed categories like mezzanine capital (Vernimmen, 2018):[1]

- For example, a detailed analysis of the various instruments of debt financing, such as credit lines, syndicated loans, or bonds, has so far received little attention in a few studies. We must criticise this, as the discussion of capital structure research clearly includes debt heterogeneity, such as covenant structures and subordination schemes (Rauh & Sufi, 2010).
- However, scientists are devoting themselves to answering this research question. Denis and Mihov (2003), for example, show that the borrower's credit quality influences the choice of debt capital source. The authors assume that creditworthiness determines a ranking when using financing sources. Companies with a high credit quality use the public capital market, while medium-quality companies resort to bank loans, and companies with a low credit quality obtain capital from investors in the private debt market (Denis & Mihov, 2003).

Consequently, the discussion of behaviour issues, structural supply-side themes, and the characteristics of different financial instruments provides additional motivation for studying capital structure. However, given these findings from a variety of areas or viewpoints, it is becoming increasingly difficult to get a comprehensive structural understanding from capital structure research. Table 1.1 summarises the findings and provides additional guidance.

1.4 Empirical Insights into Financial Decision-Making

According to Modigliani and Miller (1958), the capital structure of a company is irrelevant to its enterprise value. The value of a company with unleveraged financing is equal to the value of its equity capital, whereas in the case of a leveraged company, it is made up of the value

Table 1.1 Overview of the different theoretical stages in capital structure research in the development of capital structure theory

Stage/theme of research	*Core statement*
Capital structure irrelevance theorem (Modigliani & Miller, 1958)	Other factors, besides capital costs, do not determine the capital structure. We obtain the result under very simplistic assumptions.
Modigliani-Miller theorem with taxes (Modigliani & Miller, 1963)	The firm cannot derive an optimal capital structure with the introduction of taxes that result in beneficial tax shields (Brusov et al., 2022, p. 59).
Trade-off theory (Brennan & Schwartz, 1984; Brusov et al., 2022, p. 59; Leland, 1994)	The costs of capital, under the assumption of positive tax shields (deductibility of capital costs), and the costs of financial distress, or bankruptcy costs determine the capital structure. There are single-period and multi-period theories, as well as static and dynamic trade-off theories.
Neo-institutional theories regarding the capital structure	Agency costs, specifically those associated with asymmetric information, determine the firm's capital structure. This leads to monitoring costs, bonding costs, and a residual loss (Jensen & Meckling, 1976).
Signalling theory	According to neo-institutional theories, it can be interpreted as a problem-solving mechanism for asymmetric information. There are numerous types of signals that can be derived from the capital structure (e.g., Masulis, 1983; Ross, 1977).
Pecking order theory (Myers & Majluf, 1984)	Based on the different costs of asymmetric information that accompany different types of capital, managers chose the capital structure in a particular order, starting with cheap internal capital first and ending with the most expensive (new) equity capital.

(*Continued*)

Table 1.1 (Continued)

Stage/theme of research	*Core statement*
Market timing theory	Based on empirical findings, the market timing theory states that managers select a particular type of capital according to current market conditions.
Behavioural approaches	Focus on the influence of personality characteristics, life experiences, etc. of CEOs or managers on the capital structure (Malmendier et al., 2011). Also, the theme of overconfidence is frequently mentioned (Voon et al., 2020).
Market restrictions on the supply of capital	Includes restrictions or impediments in line with current market conditions, regulatory requirements, the size of a company, or some other firm characteristics that can impact the capital structure (e.g., Campello et al., 2010; Faulkender & Petersen, 2006).
Characteristics of the financing instruments	Focus on the impact of different types of financing instruments and on their influence on capital structure decisions, like regarding the choice of loan covenants or debt structures (e.g., Denis & Mihov, 2003; Rauh & Sufi, 2010).

Source: Own presentation.

of the equity and debt capital employed. Thus, if two companies generate the same operating profit and differ only in their capital structure, so that, in well-functioning markets, two investments with identical cash flows have the same price, the value of the leveraged company must be equal to the value of the unleveraged one. On the contrary, the expected return on equity increases as the level of debt rises; however, the risk increases at the same time. Thus, optimising the capital structure means minimising capital costs while maximising firm value by leveraging investments. Therefore, the optimal debt-to-equity ratio should maximise profitability (Kebewar, 2013). Hence, capital structure research should examine the effects of capital structure on profitability and firm growth.

However, research on the relationship between capital structure and firm performance provides ambiguous results. Thus, several studies provide indications for a negative leverage-profitability relationship:

- Eriotis et al. (2002) analysed a sample of companies from various industries for a two-year period, finding a negative effect of the debt-to-equity ratio on firm profitability. They conclude that companies that prefer internal financing for investment activities are more profitable than those that prefer debt capital for capital expenditures. However, it's important to note that internal financing often faces internal competition within the firm, with limited internal funds allocated to various investment projects (Stein, 1997).

- Frank and Goyal (2015) point out an inverse relationship between leverage and profitability, while also distinguishing firms based on their active or passive approach to adjusting their capital structure as a result of changes in profitability.
- Goddard et al. (2005) examine a sample including manufacturing and service companies from several European countries, finding a negative relationship between leverage and profitability. Instead, they find that companies with higher liquidity tend to be more profitable, which indicates that internal financing increases profitability.
- Yoon and Jang (2005) find that firm size is a stronger predictor for the ROE of firms than leverage, as well as a firm size effect in the form that larger firms show higher equity returns. The authors derived their findings from restaurant business firms.
- Rao et al. (2007) examine listed companies, finding a negative relationship between leverage, ROA, and ROE. Moreover, the authors conclude that liquidity level, firm age, and capital intensity have a significant effect on the ROE and ROA.
- Zeitun and Tian (2014) examine a sample of 167 companies for the period 1989–2003, finding a negative effect of leverage on the price-to-book ratio and revenue growth. Tobin's Q, a measure of market performance, also exhibits a negative effect.
- Ramachandra and Nageswara Rao (2008) find an association between higher leverage and lower income growth and revenue growth as a result of industry downturns. Moreover, tightening financial conditions in downturn periods are more likely to negatively affect smaller firms than larger ones.
- Nunes et al. (2009) examine Portuguese service industry companies, finding that firm size is a better predictor for firm growth and profitability within larger firms that show higher growth and display a lower level of leverage and higher profitability.
- Among a cross-industry sample from the Pakistan stock exchange, Muhammad et al. (2014) find negative relationships between debt-to-asset ratios and variables of firm performance like ROA and ROE. The authors conclude that capital structure variables have a significant impact on firm efficiency and profitability, so managers should optimise the capital structure.
- Kebewar (2013) uses a sample of 2,000 unlisted service companies, finding no relationship between profitability and leverage.

- Kuehnhausen and Stieber (2014), as well as Mwambuli (2016), also find a negative relationship between leverage and profitability, as well as with firms' liquidity.

Moreover, other research finds no effect on firm performance, such as in the studies from Baum et al. (2006) or Chadha and Sharma (2015). Based on these findings of negative and neutral effects, it can be concluded that capital structure decisions are an important factor for financial performance, but not in the sense suggested by the irrelevance theorem. Instead, most of the research finding negative or neutral effects concludes that managers shall not use excessive leverage but should fund their investment activities with internal sources, such as retained earnings, and should use leverage only as the last resort, which also supports the pecking order theory assuming that managers prefer internal financing over external financing per se.

Other research provides indications for positive effects:

- Frank and Goyal (2003) examine a broad cross-industry sample of US firms using financial data from an 18-year period. They find that the pecking order theory cannot be supported by empirical data. Instead, they found a strong positive effect of leverage on revenue growth and operating cash flow growth, supporting the trade-off theory.
- Baum et al. (2006) find for a 12-year period (1988–2000) that short-term debt has a positive effect on firm growth.
- Nguyen and Ramachandran (2006) also find a positive effect of short-term debt on firm growth, particularly among high-growth companies with a high demand for increasing working capital, concluding that profitability increases when short-term liabilities are preferred over long-term liabilities.
- Berger and Bonaccorsi di Patti (2006) find that higher leverage is associated with higher profitability in analysing a sample of US banks. Moreover, more efficient companies use higher leverage, as higher efficiency generates a higher return, which reduces financial distress and bankruptcy risks, and therefore capital costs.
- The research by Tsuruta (2017) as well as Simerly and Li (2000) supports the findings and conclusions of Fosu (2013), finding that leverage increases and drives firm performance in the short term. The increasing financial leverage also decreases the robustness towards external shocks, competition, and business cycle dynamics.
- Weill (2008) finds that the relationship between performance and leverage varies across countries, concluding that context factors influence the debt-to-equity ratio, such as bank credit access and the legal system's efficiency. The inclusion of macroeconomic exogenous variables, which opens up a new dimension that has so far been neglected in

capital structure mainstream research, explains, for example, the different types of financing behaviour in Germany, preferring the use of internal funding in a significant manner over external capital sources (Ziebarth, 2013, p. 29).
- Fosu (2013) shows that a higher leverage allows companies to use more aggressive competition strategies but that, in turn, the increased competition leads to decreasing unit prices, assuming that leveraged highly competitive market strategies can prove to be disadvantageous in the long term. He concludes that leverage allows aggressive strategies but leads to higher vulnerability.

In summary, the discussed research provides no clear evidence for the role of leverage in performance and profitability. On the one hand, debt increases when the investment volume exceeds the company's internal funding capacity, and vice versa. Furthermore, we can assume that companies with higher profitability typically have a capital structure with less leverage, despite having higher credit ratings and larger sizes.

Other studies focus on more complex relationships between capital structure and performance.

- Baum et al. (2006) found a non-linear relationship, but they did not find a significant and/or strong relationship between leverage and firm performance in terms of profitability.
- Margaritis and Psillaki (2010) find a non-linear relationship between leverage and firm performance, finding an inverse U-shaped relationship, implying that very low leverage as well as very high leverage can lead to an increase in firm performance.
- When examining 9,100 French companies from different industries, Kebewar (2012) provides evidence for a negative correlation between profitability and leverage up to a certain threshold, after which the effect reverses. They concluded that we should select quantile regression methodology instead of regression models to examine the U-shaped relationship.

A word of caution is also required regarding the general applicability of the empirical findings. Researchers studying what affects capital structures have shown that country-specific factors can have a big effect on certain balance sheet ratios in the context of each country. Below, we will highlight a few key discoveries from studies that take into account global variations in capital structure:

- Using data from emerging markets, Al-Najjar (2013) demonstrates that firms with a strong hold in jurisdiction and lower levels of shareholder protection have higher levels of cash. This, in turn, could potentially influence the firm's capital structure and financing decisions. Therefore, we should consider these influences when interpreting the findings of studies that use data on firms from very different jurisdictions.

- According to data from Serbia, Kuč and Kaličanin (2021) show that country-specific determinants play a role in firms' capital structure. The authors specifically point out the influence of inflation and the development state of the banking sector.
- Wald (1999) investigates capital structure differences on a country-by-country basis, using global data on a number of firms from developed markets, including the United States, Japan, Germany, France, and the United Kingdom. The author finds evidence for a rather similar level of leverage but uncovers differences regarding the correlation between certain capital structure ratios and other variables, including profitability and firm growth. He attributes these differences to tax differences and agency problems, which change from country to country.
- According to Wald (1999), differences in laws and institutions do matter for businesses in developed countries around the world. The work of Psillaki and Daskalakis (2009), which looked at small- and medium-sized businesses in the European Union, supports this finding in general. The authors show that factors specific to French, Italian, Greek, and Portuguese firms also influence the choice of capital structure. However, despite the relevance of country-specific determinants, firm-specific determinants play a clear role in capital structure choice, which is even more dominant in its impact.

This book will present the findings with clear implications for the empirical approach. The literature asserts that country-specific determinants influence capital structure decisions and other relevant interactions, such as profitability and growth, suggesting that a single-country focus could yield more accurate results on the topic. Furthermore, it is important to acknowledge the existence of differences across international data when comparing and interpreting empirical results from country-specific data with results from the literature that uses data from different countries. However, while the consideration of country-specific differences provides the advantages mentioned so far, it also risks preventing generalised conclusions that are applicable across a broad set of firms from different jurisdictions as well. In any case, this trade-off highlights the importance of carefully and equitably interpreting the results, a process that this monograph intends to apply to the empirical data later.

Note

1 The pecking order theory provides a counterexample to this claim, as debt is at least considered in two different forms. However, the pecking order theory does not address all potential layers of capital that are theoretically available for a firm's financing opportunities.

2 Theories and Literature Review of Business Performance

2.1 Examining Business Performance and Growth Dynamics

Various metrics, such as accounting, is used to measure performance (Quon et al., 2012). These include profitability metrics, such as the return on a firm's assets or equity. However, we can measure business performance either quantitatively or qualitatively (Bulut & Can, 2013). Given the broad nature of the concept of performance, which encompasses both qualitative and quantitative aspects, it is not surprising that academic studies on firm performance often lack a clear definition and conceptualisation of performance (Miller et al., 2013; Taouab & Issor, 2019). This problem also extends to the distinction between business performance and firm performance, as these terms are either not clearly defined and differentiated or referred to with notions of efficiency, competitiveness, value creation, or growth (Ma, 2000; Porter, 1991, 1996). The direct relationship between growth and the concept of performance, evident in the lifecycle of firms from their foundation to expansions and ultimately to necessary restructurings, makes it of particular interest (Swaay et al., 2015).

In light of this background, it is imperative to present a comprehensive analysis of business performance. To achieve this goal, it is considered useful to focus on growth as a key component of performance. This is because there are numerous areas to evaluate growth, such as revenue growth or profitability. Additionally, a quantitative approach necessitates performance measurement, allowing for the practical application of growth metrics. Furthermore, we will not distinguish between the concepts of firm performance and business performance, given their common usage in the academic literature.

With respect to the research on firm growth or business growth, a larger number of concepts and models exist, even at the level of the research object. Most researchers define firm growth in terms of the objectives of their studies, their examination subjects, and the methodology used (Schmalen et al., 2006). Consequently, different types of observed

DOI: 10.4324/9781003545194-3

growth and their implementation typically contribute to our understanding of growth. Table 2.1 provides an indication of the vast domain in which we can conceptualise firm growth. The table also displays several classification criteria and the corresponding types of growth. It is worth noting that the growth dimensions shown below are both qualitative and quantitative. This is a distinction that has implications with respect to the evaluation of business performance (Bulut & Can, 2013).

Firm growth research differs from turnaround and restructuring research in that it examines the effect of different factors on firm growth over a longer observation period than restructuring or turnaround research (Gruenwald, 2016). In its most comprehensive form, we can define factors explaining firm growth as elements (factors and resources) that consistently cause or produce firm performance (success) in any business (Lawrimore, 2011). Thus, the goal of success factor or firm growth research is to identify factors explaining excessive firm performance (Herr, 2007), as demonstrated by the different types of growth achieved. The research focuses on identifying success factors in single functional areas within the company or at the strategic management level, as well as the effects of

Table 2.1 Conceptual domains for firm growth

Classification criteria	*Types of growth*
Character	(1) Quantitative growth; (2) qualitative growth
Intensity (annual revenue growth rate over a defined period)	(1) Diminishing growth: < 5% (3-year average) (2) Moderate/normal growth: 5% to 20% (3-year average) (3) High growth (gazelles): > 20% (3-year average) (4) Hyper growth (unicorns): > 100% (3-year average)
Dynamics	(1) Evolutionary growth; (2) revolutionary growth
Permanence	(1) Saltatory growth; (2) continuous growth; (3) sustainable growth
Form of realisation	(1) Organic growth (internal growth); (2) non-organic growth (external growth)
Nature of changes	(1) Innovative growth; (2) restructuration growth
Geography	(1) Local growth; (2) regional growth; (3) supra-regional growth; (4) domestic growth; (5) international growth
Quality	(1) Sustainable growth; (2) non-sustainable growth
Area of appearance	(1) Financial growth; (2) structural growth; (3) organisational growth; (4) strategic growth
Intensity	(1) Weak growth; (2) intensive growth, (3) high growth; (4) hyper growth
Duration	(1) Short-term growth); (2) long-term growth (longevity)

Source: Own representation based on Gruenwald, 2016; OECD, 2010; Ross & Lemkin, 2016; Bhide, 2003.

exogenous factors such as sector, industry, or other group-specific determinants. This book highlights capital structure as a specific success factor responsible for the observed growth patterns of firms.

2.2 Microeconomic Foundations of Firm Growth

Business studies, in contrast to macroeconomic studies, focus solely on firms or companies. However, economics has developed its own firm theory, known as the microeconomic theory of the firm (Negishi, 2014). In this context, the production function conceptualises the firm as an entity that transforms inputs into outputs (Walker, 2017). The firm generally pursues the goal of maximising profit. As a result, in the perspective of multiple periods, the goal is to maximise the firm's value by reacting promptly and efficiently to changing price signals from the markets (Hall & Lieberman, 2013).

In contrast to macroeconomic studies, which focus on larger entities, microeconomics focuses only on the firm's interaction with the markets, but from a more distinct perspective than business and management studies. According to microeconomic theory, market forces primarily structure the firm from the outside, leaving decisions, principal-agent problems, operations, and strategies unobserved due to the market's focus, despite their clear relevance in practice (Wiese, 2021).

According to the firm's microeconomic theory, there is a production function with only minor variations from other firms. Here, the firm exists only as long as it keeps the production costs lower than the market price (Hall & Lieberman, 2013). Thus, the firm functions as a simple production function, adjusting production and output by observing and responding to market signals (Hall & Lieberman, 2012; Walker, 2018).

In general, the company adjusts its production levels and cost structure based on demand volume and price signals. The approach to maximising profits depends on the market characteristics, such as whether it is a monopolistic or a polypolistic market. These can be characterised as follows. In a monopolistic or quasi-monopolistic market characterised by imperfect competition, the price policy can increase revenue and profit. Thus, a price increase leverages profitability but decreases market demand. And, vice versa, a price reduction results in higher sales volume but decreasing margins (Hall & Lieberman, 2013).

In contrast to the monopolistic or quasi-monopolistic market, the polypolistic market is characterised by perfect competition. The efficient market generates the given equilibrium price of supply and demand, which the individual firm cannot affect (Hirschey, 2008). To stimulate demand, the firm can influence its revenue by making price reductions below the equilibrium price up to the breakeven point. However, this reduces the firm's profitability, resulting only in quantitative growth. The only option for profitable growth (qualitative growth) is a constant cost reduction to increase operation efficiency and, thus, cost efficiency. However, lowering costs all the time could lead to a big drop in production costs below the fair market price of goods. This would increase market shares while also benefiting from scale and scope effects, making it easier to lower prices (Hall & Lieberman, 2013).

The firm's microeconomic theory aims to model private firms' decisions. In factor markets, firms ask for the production factors labour and capital in order to use them in a certain combination in the technical production process and to offer the output quantity produced. Assuming a company aims to maximise its profit per period, it employs production factors to minimise opportunity costs (Hens & Pamini, 2008). This suggests that every decrease in a production factor's quantity within an input bundle leads to a corresponding decrease in the output quantity, thereby preventing any wastage of input. The production function (technical condition of production) describes the relationship between the minimum factor combinations and the output quantity produced with them (Eichhorn & Gleißner, 2016). Of course, this understanding does not consider the potential impact of capital structure considerations. The firm's microeconomic theory employs a three-step approach to model management decisions in allocation problems, which assumes the measurement of production volumes in monetary units (not quantities) and the evaluation of output using market prices. We outline the three steps below (Rubio-Misas & Gómez, 2015; Stephan & Fischer, 2008):

Among the many (infinite) production possibilities, only the technically efficient production processes are to be considered by a profit-maximising company to achieve technological efficiency. Among the (possibly infinite) technically efficient factor input combinations, the profit-maximising firm selects only the one minimum-cost input bundle for each desired output quantity to achieve economic efficiency. From the (possibly infinite) many cost-minimum producible outputs, the company chooses the profit-maximising output bundle depending on the market prices to achieve the maximum profit.

The management's objective is to optimise the cost function, which includes fixed and variable costs that the firm incurs, and the revenue function to achieve maximum profit as defined in the cost-volume-profit function (Mowen et al., 2018; Walker, 2018). When the additional cost of an additional output unit equals the additional return, a company reaches its optimal size. In terms of accounting, this refers to the breakeven point (Stephan & Fischer, 2008). Consequently, reaching the optimal size of the company would be the rational firm growth limit, beyond which additional activities initially generate risks, such as negative returns and solvency risks. Therefore, firm growth seems to be only a rational choice up to a certain degree within the limits of profitable output possibilities.

From a theoretical perspective, growth is not a rational option as long as a company can cover all its costs, including its capital costs. This is because, as the founder of the firm theory notes, "First, as a firm gets larger, there may be decreasing returns for the entrepreneur function; that is, the costs of organising additional transactions within the firm will rise" (Coase, 1937). Thus, the marginal costs define the rational limit of firm growth because, beyond this limit, the diseconomies of scale affect profitability.

In summary, the microeconomic theory of the firm focuses on optimal asset allocation based on market forces, minimising the impact of management activities on the results (Walker, 2017). However, managerial economics uses the firm's microeconomic theory as a theoretical basis for reflection and discussion of management decisions, not as a strict guide for decision-making. This approach is a response to the lack of an explicit theory of the firm in business studies and management science (Walker, 2017). Given that neither management nor business administration science has developed an explicit theory of the firm, one could interpret this approach as a response to the lack of discussion surrounding this concept. However, managerial economics employs a variety of models, including microeconomic-based ones, without explicitly referencing microeconomic theory as its core paradigm. Instead, it views microeconomic theory as one of several competing theories and models for rational management decision-making within the context of rational decision-making and management (Walker, 2017). Therefore, microeconomic theory provides a useful theoretical background for understanding the nature of firms, for example, with respect to growth mechanisms. Indeed, when neglecting uncertainty, financial economics is basically an exercise in microeconomic theory (Campbell et al., 1997).

2.3 Models of Business Growth

There are types of growth models that are more specific than the simple growth model of microeconomics. In this paragraph, we will introduce these models and evaluate them based on the research objectives. Let's start by discussing the so-called stochastic theory. This growth model assumes that there are no identifiable success factors to achieve performance except for a multitude of factors that are generating firm growth. As a result, the contribution of individual factors to success is small and therefore not measurable. Therefore, Gibrat's law, which defines growth as a stochastic process (e.g., Evans, 1987; Bottazzi & Secchi, 2003; Reichstein & Dahl, 2004; Knudsen et al., 2017), precludes the observation of performance in principle. Stochastic theories cannot explain the stochastic nature of the capital structure's contribution to growth in the context of this monograph.

Deterministic models of corporate growth, in contrast to the stochastic view of growth, assume that there are few observable internal and external factors that can explain firm growth. This view generally understands corporate growth as essentially following a management intention (Schwenker & Spremann, 2008). This paradigm forms the basis of what are probably the two most frequently cited theoretical approaches, the resource-based view and the market-based view. Following the resource-based view (RBV), such as new research on high-growth companies, resource-based models think that a company's growth depends on creating resources that are unique to the company and not available on the market. These resources are called "company-specific resources." The company's property and access to these resources distinguish it from other companies, which do not have an equal position. Thus, resource access can be used to realise a competitive advantage (e.g., Penrose, 1959; Wernerfelt, 1984; Hamel & Prahalad, 1994; Gellweiler, 2018).

In contrast to the resource-based view, the market-based view (MBV) models assume that companies grow through positioning or market-product strategies, enabling them to increase the market, which, in turn, results in benefits from scale effects (e.g., Drucker, 1954; Ansoff, 1965; Porter, 1980; Buzzell et al., 1975; Buzzell & Gale, 1989; Barney, 1991; Davidsson et al., 2002; Barringer & Jones, 2004; Davidsson & Delmar, 2006; Malik, 2008). In this respect, the right choice of strategy in terms of positioning, corporate strategy, and operations management activities is at the forefront of the explanation of firm growth, as represented by the strategic management concepts of, for example, Drucker (1954), Ansoff (1965, 1988), Kotler (1999), and particularly Porter (1980, 2008). In this sense, companies can exhibit large growth and strong performance if they are able to successfully acquire valuable core competencies (Hamel & Prahalad, 1990).

While resource-based growth models basically identify essential success factors, namely core competences (Hamel & Prahalad, 1990), company-specific resources, and market positioning (close market niche and deep customer relationship; Müller, 2013), market-based approaches and strategic management models are more strongly based on a dynamic adaptation of the firm to its corporate context (sales and procurement markets and other environmental factors), corporate structure (organisation and governance), and strategy content. An essential study from the market-based perspective is the Profit Impact of Market Strategy (PIMS) study, which, similar to Porter's approach, is rooted in industrial economics, from which Porter also derives his concept of generic strategies (Salonen, 2010). The aim of the PIMS project is to investigate the connection between corporate strategy and corporate performance and the generalisation of this connection to controllable variables based on the evaluation of the data of numerous companies from various industries and competitive situations. The ROI is often selected as an indicator of firm performance research, as is the case in the PIMS studies. Analysing the current PIMS database, Malik (2008)) refers to the PIMS dataset, which has been further supplemented over the decades. These data list a total of 15 independent variables that are condensed into three factor groups:

1. Competitive strength is defined as an aggregated factor of absolute market share, relative market share, customer preferences, patents, and segment-specific orientation.
2. Lean production measured as chapter turnover, capacity utilisation, productivity, and the ratio of external to internal production.
3. Market attractiveness with the indicators market growth, market concentration, degree of innovation, bargaining power, and logistics efficiency.

The factors mentioned above explain about 75% of the variance of the ROI (Malik, 2008), with quality and market share having the highest effect, while a high investment intensity in the context of a very low market share has a strong negative effect. These findings provide strong evidence for the ability of deterministic growth models to explain much of a firm's realised business performance.

There are also other theories on growth as an indicator of business performance. These include theories with a learning perspective that stress the importance of knowledge acquisition and learning as a key prerequisite for growth and performance (Senge, 1990; Hamel & Prahalad, 1990; Deakins & Freel, 1998; Dalley & Hamilton, 2000; Bessant et al., 2005; Phelps et al., 2007). Another viewpoint is the evolutionary perspective, which states that firm growth occurs in an environment of adaptation to competitive market dynamics (Alchian, 1950a; Penrose, 1959; Aldrich, 1999; Vinnell & Hamilton, 1999; Kaldasch, 2012).

Additionally, there is a perspective that focuses on a firm's lifecycle. Here, we explain the growth and performance dynamics by referencing a specific stage of a firm's lifecycle. This perspective largely claims that companies develop from small businesses to more mature firms, thereby exhibiting different growth dynamics throughout this development process (Churchill & Lewis, 1983; Scott & Bruce, 1987; Greiner, 1998; Dobbs & Hamilton, 2007).

Therefore, it is crucial to note that various factors have the potential to explain business performance in terms of growth. As outlined in Table 2.2., there are different theoretical approaches that aim to explain growth dynamics. What is generally missing in this research is the notion of the relevance of the capital structure. This creates an open issue in the research on growth dynamics and performance.

Table 2.2 Theoretical approaches to firm growth

Growth theory approach	*Selected authors*	*Key characteristics*
Stochastic perspective	Bottazzi and Secchi (2003) Reichstein and Dahl (2004) Gibrat (1931) Evans (1987)	Growth is assumed to depend on numerous factors that cannot be directly measured or observed.
Resource-based approach	Schumpeter (1934) Wernerfelt (1984) Hamel and Prahalad (1994) Gellweiler (2018)	Growth is a result of various internal and external factors. The determining factors are recognisable and provides a competitive advantage.
Market-based view	Ansoff (1965) Porter (1980) Barney (1991) Davidson et al. (2002) Hamel and Prahalad (1990)	Firm growth is primarily due to superior market positioning, with core competencies being critical.
Learning perspective	Senge (1990) Hamel and Prahalad (1990) Deakins and Freel (1998)	The acquisition of knowledge and a continuous learning process are mentioned as prerequisites for achieving growth.
Evolutionary perspective	Vinnell and Hamilton (1999) Kaldasch (2012) Alchian (1950a) Penrose (1959) Aldrich (1999)	Companies achieve growth by adapting to the challenges imposed by competitors and the environment.
Lifecycle perspective	Dobbs and Hamilton (2007) Scott and Bruce (1987) Greiner (1972, 1998) Churchill and Lewis (1983)	The current lifecycle of a firm influences the dynamics of company growth.

Source: Own presentation.

It is worth mentioning that there is also some academic research that combines existing approaches to growth theory. For instance, the resource-based view, which has been expanding in recent years, forms the basis of a special field of research that examines high-growth companies. The results of this research reveal, for instance, that (1) fast-growing companies often have a higher debt ratio; (2) smaller companies grow faster due to higher efficiency in more flexible, informal structures (López-Garcia & Puente, 2009); (3) fast-growing companies typically appear in later stages among smaller to medium-sized companies rather than in the start-up stage; (4) higher innovation intensity explains the rapid growth of small firms, while larger firms tend to take fewer risks and, therefore, focus on incremental innovation (e.g., Acs et al., 2008; Coad & Rao, 2010).

Two other current studies have developed very similar growth predictor models that originate from comparable samples. For comparable periods, both have analysed the financial data of German-, Austrian-, and Swiss-listed companies (569 companies and 588 companies, respectively). Wehrmann (2018) analyses 569 German, Austrian, and Swiss-listed companies, searching for the effects of internationalisation on firm growth. Gruenwald (2016) analyses the financial data of 588 listed German companies in a ten-year period (2003–2013), searching for growth predictors for small- and mid-cap companies. He finds that leveraged investment in research and development (R&D) and in property, plant, and equipment (PPE) explains net income growth as well as quantitative growth in terms of revenue growth (Gruenwald, 2016). In the case of qualitative growth, investments in PPE and R&D have a significant impact on asset turnover and increase the profitability of asset use (as indicated by the ROA) through intangible asset growth. Conversely, an increase in asset efficiency, or asset turnover growth, is the sole cause of quantitative growth. Moreover, qualitative growth firms show a significantly higher use of debt capital and intangible asset growth (Gruenwald, 2016). The main difference between quantitative and qualitative growth is that qualitative growth makes use of leverage, particularly for R&D and PPE investment (Gruenwald, 2016; Wehrmann, 2018). Wehrmann, 2018, does not identify other indicators, such as merger or acquisition activities and internationalisation strategies, as contributing to growth and, therefore, to performance.

2.4 Empirical Research on Business Performance

Below, the empirical firm performance research will be evaluated. Generally, this is related to the issue of firm growth, which needs to be mentioned as a key area for research on performance in general. Also, the research on change management and corporate restructuring will be evaluated, as it is related to performance research as well. Within these paragraphs, specific characteristics of firms relevant to their performance (e.g., size) are emphasised, as such characteristics will need to be considered in the empirical part of the thesis as well.

Henrekson and Johansson (2010) conducted a meta-analysis to summarise the state of research on employment effects in high-growth companies. The authors reviewed 28 high-growth studies, identifying several high-growth predictors, such as innovativeness, technology intensity, higher leverage, and other factors. According to López-Garcia and

Puente (2009), high-growth companies have a higher long-term debt ratio, while young, fast-growing companies have significantly higher productivity. Amat and Perramon (2010) stated that quality management significantly distinguishes high-growth companies from other companies. Almus (2000) stated that high-growth companies are mainly technology-intensive. According to Acs et al. (2008) and Hölzl (2009), younger companies grow faster due to size-related efficiency advantages, but they are less productive than mature companies.

To summarise, high-growth companies have a lower average firm age. However, this does not necessarily mean that such companies are start-ups. 70% of the companies with above-20% revenue growth in a three-year period are older than four years (Acs et al., 2008). Companies that have doubled their revenue in the three-year period show an average age of 25 years and exist longer than five years (Anyadike-Danes et al., 2009). Moreover, other findings show that high-growth companies are generally not start-ups or technology companies (Almus, 2000; Acs et al., 2008; Hölzl, 2009; Coad et al., 2014). Therefore, we can assume that mature firms can also achieve a relatively large growth rate.

However, high-growth research does have a particular focus on smaller firms because they generate the majority of innovations in contrast to larger and more mature companies, preferring less-risky investments and, therefore, showing less innovativeness but more predictable revenues (Robbins et al., 2000). Consequently, academic research searches for firm growth

Table 2.3 Research examples on predictors for high growth

Authors	*Growth/performance predictor*
Olson and Bokor (1995)	Innovation, strategic planning
Chaganti et al. (2002)	Leadership style, strategic planning, and performance controlling
Freel and Robson (2004)	Positive influence of product innovation on different growth measures, like turnover growth and profit margin growth
Wiklund and Shepherd (2003)	Growth aspiration, access to venture, and debt capital as well as human capital
Barringer et al. (2005)	Clearly defined mission (commitment to growth), customer knowledge, ability of inter-organisational cooperation
Tomczyk et al. (2013)	Personal values of entrepreneurs
Vickers and Lyon (2014)	Fit between entrepreneur's capabilities to firm strategy
Milosevic and Bass (2017)	Influence of dynamic capabilities of high-growth firms (degree of installed routines and organisational knowledge develop growth)
Barringer and Jones (2004)	Addition of managerial capacity to administer growth options

Source: Own presentation.

predictors in the field of high-growth SMEs compared to more mature firms (Siegel et al., 1993). However, such studies often use rather vaguely defined research constructs, such as growth aspiration, entrepreneur characteristics, and other qualitative factors. Table 2.3. presents a selected overview of predictors for high growth and performance from the high-growth literature.

The research examples on the performance predictors shown above hint at the existence of a large variety of potential predictors from very different fields. In empirical research, some of these predictors are difficult to measure and operationalise. Researchers describe this as a practical problem when conducting quantitative research. Therefore, it is crucial to assess research that gathers and operationalises variables and data with greater certainty, emphasising concrete facts over soft data (Dobbs & Hamilton, 2007). This study also begins by relying solely on financial data and ratios to scrutinise management decisions and activities, utilising advanced financial analysis research methods. However, the emphasis on measurement does not necessarily disregard qualitative aspects in the pursuit of growth predictors; rather, it concentrates on quantifiable variables. For instance, Fadahunsi's (2012) work offers a collection of 23 qualitative variables that are generally simple to measure. Table 2.4. provides an overview of selected research that uses measurable factors to predict firm growth.

Before we go any further, it's important to note that business research doesn't always make a clear distinction between turnaround management and restructuring management. Both terms often refer to the same management tasks in practice. However, examining both terms from a process perspective reveals that restructuring activities trigger a turnaround, during which certain indicators begin to exhibit a positive trend (Eichner, 2010).

Regarding the impact of turnaround and restructuring activities on corporate success, there has been a steady increase in empirical research since the 1970s, not only in distressed companies but also in non-distressed corporate restructurings and reorganisations (Rau, 2008). New research looking at both non-distressed corporate restructurings (turnaround) (e.g., Seward, 2016) and restructuring of distressed companies (e.g., Buschmann, 2006; Eichner, 2010; Hartmann, 2016) has been able to dig deeper into the restructuring process than ever before. This is because international standardisation of accounting and reporting for a growing number of companies since 2006 has made the data more consistent and simple to compare. In a recent study on German companies, Hartmann (2016) identified eight success-relevant restructuring strategies through an extensive literature analysis and empirical research on the restructuring strategies of listed DACH companies. These strategies include an increase in asset turnover, divestiture, CAPEX reduction, working capital reduction, debt reduction,

Table 2.4 Overview of selected studies on firm growth factors

Authors	*Findings on firm growth factors*	*Sample, region, and period*
Almus (2000)	In the group of the 10% fastest-growing companies, knowledge-based service providers and technology companies do not show a significantly share than "old economy" companies.	Active and non-active companies Region: Germany (1990–1999)
Anyadike-Danes et al. (2009)	6% of the total population of all existing companies comprises high-growth companies (average growth of more than 20%). 70% of high-growth companies exist at least 5 years.	Existing small- and medium-sized enterprises. Region: United Kingdom (1998–2008)
López- Garcia and Puente (2009)	High-growth companies use more leverage, resulting in relatively more long-term debt.	Existing small- and medium-sized enterprises. Region: Spain (1996–2003)
Amat and Perramon (2010)	Quality management, innovation focus, and pro-active human resource management are key success factors, as well as conservative, long-term oriented financial management.	Existing SME Region: Spain (1994–2007)
Daunfeldt et al. (2010)	Young growth companies create proportionally more jobs than older ones. The group of larger growth companies generated higher percentage growth.	Meta study, including the data of 28 studies on high-growth companies Region: European countries, United States, Canada (2003–2008)
Koski and Pajarinen (2011)	Subsidies are not critical to the growth of companies in the sample but are important in the start-up phase. Therefore, the assumption is that subsidies and loans increase the probability of establishing start-ups.	The 10% of the fastest-growing start-up companies from the group of all companies. Region: Finland (2003–2008)
Senderovitz et al. (2015)	Companies with a broad market strategy grow faster and more profitable than companies focusing on niche markets. Strategic orientation is the most determining factor for high growth.	Small, fast-growing companies Region: Denmark. (2010–2014)
Li et al. (2019)	High growth is driven by higher leverage	Small, fast-growing companies Region: 15 EU countries (2011–2012)

Source: Own presentation.

acquisition, OPEX reduction, and revenue increase (Hartmann, 2016). Hartmann (2016) and Eichner (2010) both say that a distressed company has a negative ROIC in the first year of the observation period. They also assert that a five-year observation period is necessary, as this is the typical duration of a restructuring or reorganisation process. As a result, this research is based on both the research period and the set of strategies mentioned above.

Asset Turnover Increase (Sales Increases): We assume that short-term sales growth strategies, such as through marketing and pricing policies, are generally relevant to success. An increase in sales leads to an increase in capital turnover. According to Nothardt (2001), the asset turnover formula also indicates an increase in the asset turnover rate, indicating that sales growth strategies in turnaround management increase the return on capital employed. Hartmann (2016) and Nothardt (2001) determine a significant influence of capital turnover on restructuring success. Management activities aimed at increasing sales and the resulting asset turnover have a more significant influence on turnaround success than, for example, cost reduction (Buschmann, 2006).

Acquisitions aim to achieve synergistic effects that lead to higher productivity, efficient resource use, and/or cost efficiency. However, only larger companies can apply this approach. Acquisitions are typically cost-intensive and require extensive financial resources. It can, therefore, be difficult for smaller companies to spend the necessary financial resources (Rocca et al., 2011), with the general positive effect of acquisitions – particularly in a shorter period – being questionable (Castrogiovannia & Bruton, 2000).

Divestment (Downsizing): The general objective of divestments is to generate an inflow of additional liquidity that will enable the company to reduce the financial shortage to finance restructuring activities (Sudarsanam & Lai, 2001). However, according to Kane and Richardson (2002, p. 260), risk assessment may also be decisive for divestment. For instance, when a business unit faces specific risks, a divestment can mitigate the risk and decrease the volatility of operating cash flow and costs. Empirical studies show a positive correlation between divestments and turnaround success, with the exception of Sudarsanam and Lai (2001), who found a negative, non-significant correlation between the sale of assets and turnaround success. Eichner (2010), Naujoks (2012), and Schmuck (2012) find a significant positive correlation between divestments and restructuring success.

CAPEX: Eichner (2010) finds no significant relationship between the reduction and increase in investments and restructuring success. Buschmann (2006) finds a negative but not significant relationship between CAPEX reduction and firm performance. Buschmann (2006) argues that, although successful companies initially reduce CAPEX, they must invest significantly more in the following years to achieve long-term corporate success.

OPEX: Sudarsanam and Lai (2001) consider a reduction in costs to be relevant to success, especially in the initial phase of the turnaround process. Overall, the relevance of cost reduction measures seems to be high, especially in the initial phase of the turnaround process (Robbins & Pearce, 1992), since this phase is about stopping the decline in the company's performance, stabilising it, and, thus, securing its survival by increasing the cash flow. Buschmann (2006) finds a positive but non-significant correlation between cost reduction and turnaround success. Castrogiovanni and Bruton (2000) find no significant relationship. Studies that have identified a negative correlation between cost reduction and turnaround performance, such as Morrow et al. (2004), find a negative but non-significant correlation between cost reduction and ROI in growing industries. Naujoks (2012) finds a negative, non-significant correlation between cost reduction and turnaround success.

Working capital: Improving working capital is one way to improve a company's financial situation in the relatively short term (Bibeault, 1999). Inadequate control of working capital can even be a reason for a company's decline in performance (Grinyer et al., 1988). Reducing working capital reduces the amount of capital tied up in a company. As a result, the company releases financial resources (Meyer, 2007). You can then use the released funds for turnarounds or new investments. Bergauer (2001) emphasises the importance of leveraging liquidity with creditor and debtor management as the primary positive effect on change management and turnarounds. However, the effect depends on the company's size. Howorth and Westhead (2003) point out that for small companies, strict and organised working capital management has a much greater effect on turnaround performance. Small companies need to control working capital, as they generally have a comparatively higher proportion of short-term assets, lower liquidity, higher cash flow volatility, and greater dependence on short-term debt than more mature and older companies (Howorth & Westhead, 2003).

Debt Reduction: A high debt-to-equity ratio and the associated high interest payments can influence a company's funding ability (Pant, 1991). However, an increase in the debt ratio can enable necessary growth spurts and restructuring. Naujoks (2012) finds a significant positive correlation between the reduction of the debt ratio and turnaround success. Eichner (2010) and Hartmann (2016) have no effect. Here, it is possible to assume a threshold in terms of the ratio between free cash flow and the debt-to-capital ratio, with a positive effect of a rising free cash flow on the potential to increase the debt-to-capital ratio (Damodaran, 2002).

The size of the company can have a significant impact on a turnaround's success. From a more resource-oriented perspective, Ramanujam (1984) argues that large companies are more likely to achieve a turnaround due to their larger resource base and experience. In contrast, Smith and Graves (2005) find a positive correlation between the size of a company and its turnaround success. Eichner (2010), on the other hand, finds a negative but not significant correlation between company size and turnaround success. Just as in firm growth research, restructuring/turnaround research provides the indication that firm size is a relevant control variable.

Concerning the performance indicator, Hartmann (2016) and Eichner (2010) pointed out that the existing literature contains a multitude of different concepts for turnaround and restructuring, as well as for its operationalisation in research. Note that there is a common understanding of performance criteria. In 32 empirical studies, Hartmann (2016) found at least three groups of performance criteria. However, most of the performance indicators were accounting-related, and most of the studies in this area preferred ROI or ROIC (Eichner, 2010; Hartmann, 2016). As a benchmark, restructuring is defined as successful if the company's ROIC achieves at least 7% to 9%, which is above the average risk-free interest rate of government bonds plus the risk premium of the capital market (Hartmann, 2016; Buschmann, 2006). Otherwise, the additional investment does not generate an acceptable return to justify the company's continuation.

Delmar et al. (2003) state that one-third of the studies included in their literature review use revenue growth as a growth indicator. Shepherd and Wiklund (2009) even found that two-thirds of firm growth studies use revenue as a growth metric. Achtenhagen et al. (2010, p. 293) find that almost 50% of the examined studies use revenue growth as a growth indicator, 30% use staff numbers, and 20% measure the management's growth intention. In total, 40% of the studies are only cross-sectional studies; 60% are longitudinal studies. Only 30% of the studies are based on secondary data, while 70% are based on primary data (Achtenhagen et al., 2010, p. 293), which does not allow for reproducing or comparing the results. Achtenhagen et al. (2010, p. 309) found in interviewing 2,000 Swedish CEOs a wide gap between the growth perceptions and metrics of managers and business research, concluding that growth metrics and factors in business research are mainly quantitative, whereas managers prefer to apply a lot of qualitative indicators and qualitative factors to explain firm growth.

The academic literature rarely includes quality measures. Some studies use qualitative growth indicators, such as innovation intensity increase (e.g., Beers & Zand, 2014; Frenz & Letto-Gilles, 2009). Kanji et al. (2015) assert that traditional metrics for evaluating growth and performance confine themselves to isolated aspects and lack the necessary complexity to encompass the full range of factors contributing to these outcomes. As such, there is a need for a more multifaceted approach to assessing firm growth and performance. One promising avenue is to measure performance in terms of the proportion of innovative sales to total revenue, an approach employed by recent studies such as Frenz and Letto-Gilles (2009) and Beers and Zand (2014).

However, on the one hand, there are studies that have failed to uncover any correlations between firm performance and innovation growth (e.g., Acs et al., 2008; Coad et al., 2014). Conversely, there is a suggestion that these indicators are most effective in assessing the performance of technology-driven firms and can function as dependable predictors of revenue or income growth. It is important to note, however, that innovation growth may not be an appropriate metric for evaluating firm performance across different industries (Coad et al., 2014).

In summary, current research primarily uses two indicators to measure firm growth: (1) employment growth and (2) annual turnover or sales growth, while empirical research less frequently uses profitability ratios. However, this study employs a broader range of measures to capture multiple dimensions of firm performance. Specifically, the study employs (1) revenue growth to assess quantitative growth, (2) operating income growth to evaluate qualitative growth, and (3) profitability ratios, such as ROA, ROE, or ROIC, to determine overall firm performance. This study aims to provide a more comprehensive assessment of firm performance by incorporating both traditional growth measures (i.e., revenue and employment growth) and additional indicators to differentiate between qualitative and quantitative growth, as well as the relationship between investment activities and profitability.

Achtenhagen et al. (2010) highlight the relevance of firm growth research when it integrates theory with business practice. However, academic research frequently formulates and responds to research questions that are irrelevant to management practice, or it employs definitions, concepts, and indicators that are not applicable in the practical realm of business management. Furthermore, there is no explanation or substantiation for the selection of these indicators (Achtenhagen et al., 2010).

Table 2.5 highlights the diversity of different growth indicators. For instance, one may wonder why financial analysis research rejects the ROE as a useful performance indicator, given its calculative sensitivity to moral hazards.

Table 2.5 Examples and frequency of growth indicators in empirical research

Growth indicator variable	*Percent*
Revenue (also called sales or turnover)	41.8
Number of employees	27.3
Growth intention	18.2
Profitability	7.3
Combined measures	16.4
Growth strategies	16.4

Source: Achtenhagen et al. (2010).

3 Global Perspectives on Capital Structure Decisions

3.1 Comparative Analysis of Capital Structures in Different Markets

Market organisations shape their capital structure to achieve both long-term and short-term objectives. The structure of capital takes into account both internal and external sources in a proper combination. This term is crucial to understanding how companies shape an appropriate corporate financial strategy and manage the associated risks. We can observe that the determinants of capital structure differ significantly across markets all over the world according to diverse economic environments, corporate governance practices, various tax systems, and also the conditions of the financial market they operate in. All these components are important in shaping capital structure strategy, and they influence it significantly. Based on the collected data, there is evidence that in developed markets, companies benefit from well-established financial infrastructures because they provide a wide array of financing options. They include access to deep and liquid equity markets and sophisticated debt instruments (Rajan & Zingales, 1995; Booth et al., 2001).

If enterprises have access to external sources of long-term financing characterised by attractive interest rates, this allows them to use the financial leverage effect and, at the same time, reduce the weighted average cost of capital as a whole. Developed markets typically have a robust institutional and legal structure that protects investors and ensures the fulfilment of commitments at the same time. Such conditions reduce the market risk premium associated with the use of debt while increasing the attractiveness of leverage (La Porta et al., 1998). Corporate governance practices in developed markets also have a significant impact on entities' capital structure decisions. Independent supervisory boards and stringent regulatory standards influence the effectiveness of entity management, transparency, and agency cost reduction, which makes debt financing more advantageous (Shleifer & Vishny, 1997). Additionally, tax systems in many developed countries provide incentives for the use of

DOI: 10.4324/9781003545194-4

debt financing, which further promotes higher financial leverage (Modigliani & Miller, 1963). One such option is to include interest in the financing costs, which reduces the long-term cost. Market liquidity and capitalisation levels are also important factors that influence the shape of an enterprise's potential capital structure. Large and liquid exchanges with higher market capitalisation distinguish developed markets, giving companies greater access to capital and reducing financing costs. In turn, emerging markets have smaller exchanges with lower liquidity, which results in greater volatility and challenges in obtaining financing (Duttagupta & Pazarbasioglu, 2021). Developed and emerging markets also differ in their investment risk and return profiles. Given the inverse relationship between risk and potential rate of return, the risk in developed markets is significantly lower than in developing markets. Therefore, securities traded on developed markets will be suitable for conservative investors. Emerging markets, although enable higher profits, are characterised by increased risk, including currency fluctuations and often low political stability (Deloitte China, 2023). Companies that seek to raise capital in emerging markets have to face higher debt costs and often have limited access to equity financing. According to Demirgüç-Kunt and Maksimovic (1998), the financial markets in these locations are frequently less established, more volatile, and less liquid. As a result, it is more challenging for businesses to raise capital in these regions. As a result, businesses operating in emerging markets are more likely to rely on equity capital and relatively short-term debt, which ultimately leads to lower leverage ratios. At the same time, a poorly developed institutional system, which often lacks stable legal regulations and rights enforcement, increases the risks associated with external financing. Therefore, these are factors that discourage entities from using debt (Claessens & Laeven, 2003). Moreover, the lack of excellent corporate governance practices in emerging markets leads to higher agency costs and lower investor confidence. The lack of transparency and accountability in these markets increases risks for creditors and investors, thereby limiting the availability of debt and increasing the cost of external financing (Ayyagari et al., 2010). Informal lending channels, such as trade credits and family loans, play an important role in the capital structure of enterprises in emerging markets, which are often associated with higher financing costs and shorter debt maturities (Booth et al., 2001).

Summarising the aforementioned considerations, we can state that many important factors determine the capital structure in both developing and developed markets. Understanding these differences is essential to formulating effective investment and financing strategies that align with each company's specific goals. The rest of the chapter will present the factors influencing the formation of capital structures in key global economies, which include the United States, European Union countries,

Table 3.1 Comparison of factors influencing capital structure in emerging and developed markets

Factor	*Emerging markets*	*Developed markets*
Access to capital	Limited access to capital and high financing costs	Easy access to capital and low financing costs
Economic stability	High volatility, political, and economic risk	Stable economy and low political and economic risk
Cost of capital	Higher cost of capital due to risk and uncertainty	Lower cost of capital due to stability and trust
Financial market development	Poorly developed financial markets	Highly developed financial markets
Access to information	Limited access to reliable information	Easy access to a wide range of reliable information
Ownership structure	Dominance of large investors and family owners	Diversified ownership and significant institutional share
Dividend policy	Tendency to reinvest profits	Tendency to pay regular dividends
Transaction costs	Higher transaction costs	Lower transaction costs
Law and regulations	Less developed and enforceable economic law	Stable and transparent economic law
Corruption	Higher level of corruption	Lower level of corruption
Corporate culture	Less developed corporate culture	Advanced corporate culture
Macroeconomic external factors	Greater susceptibility to external economic shocks	Greater resilience to external economic shocks
Risk management	Limited risk management capabilities	Advanced risk management strategies

Source: own elaboration

and China. Separately, we will present the impact of factors specific to each of these economies. In each of the presented world economies, we will analyse the economic situation, cultural conditions, market conditions, the applicable legal framework, and the possibilities of using financial leverage. The assessment will be based on the current literature on finance. The United States is characterised by a developed market economy with a large service and technology sector. Economic stability and a well-developed financial system favour the use of a wide range of financial instruments, including the issuance of shares, bonds, and various forms of long-term credit. Moreover, the United States has had a strong culture of entrepreneurship and innovation for many years. Enterprises are often willing to take risks, which translates into a greater willingness to use equity capital, particularly venture capital and private equity, especially in the technology sector. The US capital market is one of the most developed in the world. Easy access to capital makes companies willing to issue shares and bonds. Although regulations like the Dodd-Frank Act aim to limit excessive risk, high market liquidity also promotes greater financial leverage. The US capital market is one of the most important and developed in the world. It is also a key element of the global financial system, characterised by high liquidity, a wide range of financial instruments, and strict regulations aimed at protecting investors. It consists of many segments that enable companies to raise capital and investors to invest their funds in various financial instruments. The two largest stock exchanges in the United States are the New York Stock Exchange and NASDAQ. The New York Stock Exchange is the world's largest stock exchange in terms of the market capitalisation of the companies listed there. The second-largest stock exchange in the United States, known for listing many technology and innovative companies, is NASDAQ. The New York Stock Exchange (NYSE) is the largest stock exchange in the world, with an equity market capitalisation of over 28 trillion US dollars as of March 2024. As of February 2024, NASDAQ has a market cap of 23,414 trillion.

The US capital market has significant global importance, drawing investors from all over the world and serving as a representation of the global economy. The country's well-developed capital markets and favourable regulatory framework make it highly dependent on equity funding. Companies can reduce their dependence on borrowing by obtaining substantial amounts of equity funding from robust and highly liquid stock markets. Furthermore, the tax policy in the United States encourages debt financing by allowing the deduction of loan servicing expenses. Enterprises frequently prefer equity capital because it has a lower risk profile and provides greater flexibility for funding operations (Frank & Goyal, 2009; Graham et al., 2015). The large number of institutional investors and widespread shareholder activity in the United States further strengthen the attractiveness of financing on the capital market. They thus contribute to strengthening ethical corporate practices and further increasing market transparency. Research has shown that US corporations tend to maintain lower leverage ratios than their global counterparts, thereby emphasising financial flexibility and operational independence (Huang & Ritter, 2009).

Raising capital for businesses in the United States is a complex and diverse process, reflecting the variety of available financing sources. The financing structure of an enterprise includes both internal sources, such as retained earnings, and external sources, such as equity capital and external capital. Therefore, let us present in detail the capital structure of American enterprises.

Retained earnings are an important source of financing for many entities in the United States. Companies often reinvest their profits, which allows them to finance further development without the need to incur external liabilities. According to data collected by the Federal Reserve, retained earnings constitute approximately 30–40% of a company's total financial resources (Federal Reserve, 2022).

Because the capital market is well developed, enterprises have many opportunities to obtain external equity capital. Issuing shares is therefore one of the most popular ways of raising capital for public companies. In 2022, NASDAQ conducted approximately 156 initial public offerings (IPOs), raising capital worth approximately USD 14.8 billion (NASDAQ, 2022). In 2022, American stock exchanges conducted approximately 200 IPOs, raising capital worth approximately USD 60 billion. Furthermore, funding sources such as venture capital and private equity play an important role in financing start-ups and rapidly growing enterprises. In 2022, the value of venture capital investments in the United States was approximately USD 200 billion, while private equity investments reached USD 700 billion (PitchBook, 2022; National Venture Capital Association, 2022).

Companies in the United States also rely on external financing sources. Bank loans are therefore a traditional and common source of operational and investment financing for enterprises. The value of bank loans granted to American companies was approximately USD 2 trillion (Federal Reserve, 2022). Another important source of external financing is the issuance of corporate bonds, which constitute a significant source of long-term financing. Based on available data, the US corporate bond market is currently worth approximately USD 10.9 trillion. This value includes both investment-grade bonds and speculative bonds (high yield). The total market value is determined by new bond issuance as well as the value of bonds in circulation (Securities Industry and Financial Markets Association [SIFMA], 2024a; Federal Reserve Bank of St. Louis, 2024). In the first quarter of 2024, the issuance of investment-grade bonds reached a record high of USD 658 billion, showing significant growth compared to previous years. This increase in issuance also reflects strong demand in the US corporate bond market (Breckinridge Capital Advisors, 2024). Additional data indicate that these financial instruments trade dynamically, with a trading volume of approximately USD 50.1 billion per day in June 2024. This also indicates a high level of investor activity in this market (SIFMA, 2024b).

Leasing is another important source of capital, particularly for financing fixed assets. According to the Equipment Leasing and Finance Association, operating and finance leasing in the United States is valued at approximately USD 1 trillion per year. Trade loans, which enable deferment of payments for goods and services, account for approximately 20–25% of total operating financing for businesses (Institute for Supply Management, 2022). Enterprises in the United States also use hybrid financing, which often combines the features of both equity and external capital. One form of hybrid capital is convertible bonds, which combine the features of debt and equity. They enable enterprises to flexibly raise capital. The US convertible bond market is approximately USD 500 billion (Bloomberg, 2022). Preferred securities, which offer fixed income in the form of dividends but have limited voting rights, account for another USD 200 billion (Dealogic, 2022).

Currently, more and more innovative forms of financing are appearing on the financial market. One of them is crowdfunding, which has gained popularity, especially among start-ups and entities with innovative products. In 2022, enterprises raised approximately USD 20 billion through crowdfunding platforms (Crowdfund Insider, 2022). Enterprises also benefit from bridge capital. Mezzanine capital is a hybrid form of financing, containing features of debt and equity. It usually takes the form of a subordinated loan or bond. This capital may also exhibit characteristics of a capital investment, such as warrants or options to purchase shares of the financed company. The mezzanine financing market in the United States is valued at approximately USD 100 billion (Preqin, 2022a).

In recent years, the importance of alternative sources of financing has also increased in the United States. The issuance value of green bonds, used to finance sustainable development projects, reached approximately USD 50 billion in 2022, indicating the growing interest of companies and investors in sustainable financing of their investments (Climate Bonds Initiative, 2022). In the United States, the structure of business finance sources varies over time. Enterprises use both internal and external capital sources, tailoring their financial strategy to current market conditions, operational requirements, and investment opportunities. The rise of alternative forms of financing such as venture capital, crowdfunding, and green bonds reflects changing priorities and innovations in the financial sector.

The European Union (EU) is a political and economic union of 27 member states that cooperate at various levels to ensure coherent economic, social, and political development. The Maastricht Treaty founded the Community in 1993 with the aim of promoting economic integration and upholding peace and stability on the European continent. The European Union's internal markets create a uniform structure that allows the free movement of goods, services, capital, and people between member states. As a result, businesses can benefit from a larger sales market and allocate resources more effectively. The common currency in 19 of the 27 member states is the euro, thus creating the Eurozone. The euro's introduction facilitated international trade and investment within the zone, reducing transaction costs and exchange rate risk. The European Union pursues a common economic and fiscal policy aimed at sustainable development, economic growth, and financial stability. The European Central Bank (ECB) plays a key role in managing monetary policy. The European Union has one of the world's largest economies, accounting for approximately 15% of global GDP. A diversified economic structure, including a strong industrial sector and a developed service sector, makes the EU a key player on the international stage. Economic growth, technological innovation, and sustainable development are EU priorities that attract investors and trade partners from around the world. EU countries are experiencing varying rates of economic development. The EU economy is based on a strong industrial and service sector. The importance of sustainable development and green finance has increased in recent years (European Commission, 2020a). Corporate culture in Europe is more conservative compared to the United States. Enterprises often prefer stability and long-term relationships with banks, which translates into greater use of bank loans and corporate bonds. Moreover, EU regulations promote a responsible approach to risk management (La Porta et al., 1998). Companies in the EU tend to maintain lower levels of leverage and place greater emphasis on financial stability and sustainability.

Europe's capital markets, while developed, are more dispersed than those in the United States. Stock exchanges such as Euronext, Deutsche Börse, and the London Stock Exchange play a crucial role for companies seeking to raise capital. Raising capital by enterprises in the European Union (EU) is a multifaceted process, including both traditional and modern forms of financing. The structure of corporate financing in the EU is slightly different from that in the United States, reflecting the diversity of member states' economies and regulations.

Retained earnings play a major role in financing European companies. Companies often reinvest their profits, which allows them to develop and modernise their businesses without having to incur external liabilities. According to data from the European Central Bank (ECB), retained earnings constitute approximately 25–35% of total corporate financial resources (ECB, 2022b).

Share issuance is another important source of capital for many European entities, especially for businesses already listed on stock exchanges. European stock exchanges carried out approximately 150 IPOs in 2022, raising capital worth approximately EUR 40 billion (Euronext, 2022). Venture capital and private equity financing play an important role, especially in financing innovative start-ups. In 2022, the value of venture capital investment in the EU was approximately EUR 100 billion, while private equity reached EUR 300 billion (European Investment Fund, 2022; Invest Europe, 2022).

Venture capital and private equity also play an important role, especially in financing innovative start-ups. In 2022, the value of venture capital investment in the EU was approximately EUR 100 billion, while private equity reached EUR 300 billion (European Investment Fund, 2022; Invest Europe, 2022).

The traditional and dominant source of financing for European enterprises is bank loan. The value of bank loans granted to EU enterprises amounted to approximately EUR 5 trillion (European Central Bank, 2022a). Another important source of long-term financing are corporate bonds; it is estimated that their value in 2022 will amount to approximately EUR 3 trillion (SIFMA, 2022).

Leasing is also an important form of financing, especially for small- and medium-sized enterprises (SMEs). The EU estimates the value of operational and financial leasing at approximately EUR 300 billion annually (Leaseurope, 2022). Trade loans, which involve deferring payments for goods and services, constitute approximately 15–20% of the total operational financing of enterprises (European Payment Report, 2022).

In EU countries, hybrid financing is a flexible form of raising capital. In 2022, the estimated value of the convertible bond market in the EU was approximately EUR 200 billion (Bloomberg, 2022). The preferred securities market, which provides stable income in the form of dividends, contributed another EUR 100 billion (Dealogic, 2022).

In recent years, special forms of financing have also become more popular, especially among SMEs and start-ups. In 2022, companies in the EU raised approximately EUR 10 billion through crowdfunding platforms (Crowdfund Insider, 2022). In 2022, mezzanine financing, which combines elements of debt and equity, amounted to EUR 50 billion (Preqin, 2022a).

Similarly, as in the United States, there has been a noticeable increase in the importance of alternative sources of financing in recent years. Green bond issuance in the EU in 2022 amounted to approximately EUR 80 billion, indicating a growing interest in sustainable financing (Climate Bonds Initiative, 2022).

In summary, the European Union's enterprises have a diverse and dynamic financing structure. Enterprises use both internal and external sources of capital, adapting their financial strategies to current market conditions as well as operational and investment needs. The rise of alternative forms of financing such as venture capital, crowdfunding, and green bonds reflects changing priorities and innovations in the financial sector. The European Union, with its unique economic and political characteristics, is an important element of the global economy. Economic diversification, a conservative corporate culture, and developed but dispersed financial markets have a significant impact on companies' capital structure decisions. The increasing importance of sustainable development and green finance is further shaping capital-raising and financial management strategies in the EU, making it an attractive and innovative market for investors around the world.

China is not only the world's second-largest economy, but it is also the largest exporter and one of the largest importers of goods. The country is a key trading partner for many countries and plays a significant role in global supply chains. China is also one of the world's largest investors, engaging in infrastructure and economic projects under its "One Belt, One Road" initiative. The Chinese government plays an active role in shaping economic policy, which affects the availability of capital and financing conditions (Naughton, 2018). The capital structure of Chinese enterprises is affected by state policy that supports infrastructure, innovation, and sustainable development. High levels of domestic savings and low interest rates favour long-term investments.

Strong ties to the government and long-term planning dominate the corporate culture of enterprises in China. Enterprises often benefit from preferential bank loans and state support. Chinese business culture places significant emphasis on relationships (guanxi) and loyalty, which influences management structures and attitudes towards risk (Liu et al., 2019). As a result, Chinese companies tend to maintain higher levels of leverage by taking advantage of widely available bank loans. The Chinese capital market, with the main stock exchanges in Shanghai (SSE) and Shenzhen (SZSE), is developing quite dynamically. Government initiatives support an increase in the issuance of corporate bonds and green bonds. The Chinese government actively promotes the development of financial markets and fintech, which increases the availability of capital and innovation in the financial sector (Hsu et al., 2019). However, the strict regulation of financial markets in China influences the dynamics of capital raising. Companies in China raise capital, which is a key element of the dynamics of one of the world's fastest-growing economies. Innovative and alternative methods of raising capital complement traditional sources of financing, reflecting the unique features of China's economic system in the structure of corporate financing.

Retained earnings constitute an important source of financing for Chinese enterprises. Thanks to rapid economic growth and high profit rates, many companies decide to reinvest their funds. According to the China Banking and Insurance Regulatory Commission (CBIRC), retained earnings account for approximately 30–40% of enterprises' total financial resources (CBIRC, 2022).

A common way for Chinese companies to raise capital is by issuing shares, especially on stock exchanges in Shanghai (SSE) and Shenzhen (SZSE). In 2022, Chinese stock exchanges conducted approximately 500 IPOs, raising capital worth around USD 85 billion (Shanghai Stock Exchange, 2022). Venture capital and private equity also play an important role in financing start-ups and fast-growing companies. In 2022, venture capital investment in China was approximately USD 70 billion, while private equity reached USD 150 billion (China Venture, 2022).

Bank loans are the dominant source of financing for Chinese enterprises because of their strong banking sector and political support. China's enterprises received bank loans valued at approximately USD 20 trillion (People's Bank of China, 2022). Corporate bonds are also an important source of long-term financing. The Asian Development Bank valued the Chinese corporate bond market at approximately USD 3 trillion in 2022.

Leasing is also an increasingly common financing surrogate, especially among small- and medium-sized enterprises (SMEs). The value of the operational and financial leasing market in China is estimated at approximately USD 500 billion per year (China Leasing Alliance, 2022). Trade credits, which enable the deferment of payments for goods and services, account for approximately 15–20% of enterprises' total operational financing (PwC China, 2022).

Convertible bonds, as a hybrid form of capital raising, are also a flexible form of capital raising. The convertible bond market in China was approximately USD 100 billion in 2022 (Bloomberg, 2022), and the preferred stock market was another USD 50 billion (Dealogic, 2022).

Also noteworthy is the increasing popularity of special forms of financing. Innovative start-ups also raised capital through crowdfunding. In 2022, Chinese enterprises raised approximately USD 5 billion through crowdfunding platforms (Crowdfund Insider, 2022). Preqin (2022a) values the mezzanine market at approximately USD 30 billion.

In recent years, the importance of alternative sources of financing has also increased. In 2022, green bond issuance in China was approximately USD 100 billion, indicating a growing interest in sustainable finance (Climate Bonds Initiative, 2022).

China, thanks to its dynamic economic development, centralisation, and technological innovation, plays a key role in the global economic arena. China's unique cultural, political, and economic characteristics shape the capital structure of its enterprises. In China, the structure of enterprise financing sources is diverse and dynamic. Strong connections with the government, the active role of the state in the economy, and long-term planning influence decisions regarding capital raising and financial management. Enterprises use both internal and external sources of capital, adapting their financial strategies to current market conditions as well as operational and investment needs. The rise of alternative forms of financing such as venture capital, crowdfunding, and green bonds reflects changing priorities and significant innovation in the financial sector.

3.2 Impact of Technological Advancements on Financial Strategies

Fintech is a new financial industry that applies technology to improve financial activities (Schueffel, 2016). Another definition of technological innovations can be found here: "Fintech represents a technologically enabled financial innovation that could result in new business models, applications, processes, or products with an associated material effect on financial markets, institutions, and the provision of financial services" (Arner et al., 2015). Technological innovations, especially in the areas of fintech and blockchain, have a significant impact on the financing strategies of enterprises and their capital structure. The goal of this part of the chapter is to analyse how modern technologies affect capital raising, debt management, and capital distribution. We will also discuss the new opportunities and challenges that technology presents for maintaining an optimal capital structure. The subchapter will present practical examples of financial and technological innovations currently occurring in the world.

Technological innovations in finance are significantly influencing the way companies raise capital by offering them new financing opportunities. In recent years, there has been the development of innovative platforms and financing tools. Increasingly popular forms of obtaining financial resources by entities are crowdfunding, peer-to-peer lending, and equity platforms.

Crowdfunding is a method of raising capital in which many people invest or donate small amounts of money to finance a project, enterprise, or initiative. Online crowdfunding platforms make this process easier by linking creators with possible investors or donors. Crowdfunding has grown in popularity in recent years as an alternate source of finance for start-ups, small businesses, and social and artistic projects (Lambert & Schwienbacher, 2010; Belleflamme et al., 2014; Mollick, 2014).

Crowdfunding platforms enable companies to raise capital from a large number of small investors via the Internet. There are several crowdfunding models. One of them is reward-based crowdfunding, in which companies offer products or prizes in exchange for financial support. This method of obtaining financing is common for creative projects and innovative technological products. Examples of such platforms are Kickstarter and Indiegogo.

Another form of obtaining financing is equity-based crowdfunding, in which investors receive shares in the company in exchange for their investments. This method enables companies to raise equity capital without the need for traditional venture capitalists. Platforms that use this financing strategy include Seedrs and Crowdcube.

Debt-based crowdfunding (also known as peer-to-peer lending) is a kind of financing in which investors lend money to businesses in exchange for interest. It is an alternative to typical bank loans, often with better financing terms. Platforms that enable this type of borrowing include Funding Circle and LendingClub. The fintech industry's growth has also enabled the development of innovative lending platforms that provide businesses with rapid and simple access to financing. Platforms serve as intermediaries between borrowers and lenders in peer-to-peer lending, removing the need for traditional financial institutions. Prosper and Zopa are two examples of this type of money-raising. Platforms that are part of marketplace lending connect businesses with financial institutions and institutional investors that offer loans on a variety of terms. We can differentiate between OnDeck and Kabbage, which act as intermediaries in this type of financing.

The development of financial and technological innovations also enables the creation of investment platforms that allow enterprises to access capital through the issuance of bonds, shares, and other financial instruments. Digital investment platforms offer tools for managing investment portfolios, enabling companies to issue bonds and shares directly to investors. Such platforms include Robinhood and Betterment. In turn, as part of Security Token Offerings (STOs), companies can issue tokens representing shares in the company or other assets, which allows for quick and safe capital raising.

Blockchain technology ensures the transparency and security of transactions. Examples of such companies include Polymath and Securitize. Blockchain is revolutionising capital distribution by decentralising and tokenising assets. Companies can issue digital tokens representing company shares or other assets, making them easier to sell and transfer. Tokenisation also allows for fractional ownership, which increases liquidity and the availability of capital (OECD, 2022). Blockchain ensures transparency and immutability of financial records, which is crucial in debt management. Smart contracts enable automatic enforcement of contract terms, which reduces the risk of default and lowers transaction costs. Banks and financial institutions use blockchain to issue bonds and other debt instruments, which increases the efficiency and security of these operations (World Economic Forum, 2022).

The fintech sector also uses advanced technologies such as artificial intelligence (AI) and big data to improve the process of raising capital. Platforms using AI and big data analyse companies' financial data to assess credit risk and creditworthiness. This makes the loan verification and approval process faster and more precise. Upstart and ZestFinance are two examples of entities that operate in this manner. In turn, robo-advisors provide automated financial advice, assisting businesses in capital management and investment decision-making. Examples of such solutions include Wealthfront and Personal Capital.

As a result, fintech technological advancements are transforming the way businesses acquire funds by delivering innovative platforms and financing solutions. Thanks to technological innovations, enterprises can use various crowdfunding models, lending, and investment platforms, as well as advanced technologies such as AI and big data. These new financing options provide companies with greater flexibility, access to capital, and cost efficiency, which is particularly important for start-ups, small- and medium-sized enterprises, and innovative projects.

The forms of capital raising described here enable the direct raising of funds from retail and institutional investors, bypassing traditional financial institutions. According to the most recent data available, experts predict that the worldwide fintech sector will be worth around USD 312.92 billion by 2024. The forecasts show an increase of USD 608.35 billion by 2029, representing a compound annual growth rate (CAGR) of more than 14% from 2024 to 2029 (Mordor Intelligence, 2024; Market Data Forecast, 2024). Other sources project a slightly larger value for the fintech sector, up to USD 644.6 billion by 2029 at a CAGR of 25.18%.

The development of digital payments, investments in fintech, and the use of new technologies like blockchain, artificial intelligence (AI), and process automation are driving the growth. The sector is also expanding rapidly in Asia-Pacific, the world's fastest-growing fintech market (Fortune Business Insights, 2024). Technological innovations therefore offer numerous benefits to companies, such as greater flexibility in raising capital, reduced transaction costs, and improved financial transparency. Technologies such as blockchain and fintech also enable better risk management and increase the availability of capital for start-ups and SMEs. Despite their numerous advantages, new technologies also present obstacles. Legal restrictions frequently fall behind the rapid advancement of technology, resulting in legal confusion. Another critical concern is digital security, particularly in terms of cyberattacks and data protection. Furthermore, incorporating new technology into current financial systems can be costly and complicated (EY, 2023).

Fintech and blockchain are transforming firms' financial strategies, influencing how they generate capital, manage debt, and disperse capital. These technologies present new prospects for increasing efficiency, lowering expenses, and improving financial transparency. However, deploying these technologies presents a number of hurdles, including legislation, digital security concerns, and integration expenses. To effectively deploy new technologies in capital structure management, businesses must carefully balance the benefits and hazards.

3.3 Regulatory Influences on Capital Structure Decisions Globally

Capital structure decisions and various aspects of business operations worldwide are significantly influenced by regulatory influences. This section examines the impact of regulations on capital structure decisions in a variety of global locations.

Tax regulation is one of the most significant regulatory factors that affect the capital structure. Many countries deduct interest from their tax bases, making debt a more attractive source of financing than equity. In the United States, for example, tax benefits associated with debt may induce companies to increase the level of debt in their capital structure. Nevertheless, there are also constraints, such as thin capitalisation rules, that are designed to prevent over-indebtedness in order to reduce the tax burden. The availability and cost of debt capital are significantly influenced by banking regulations. For example, capital requirements imposed on banks, such as those resulting from the Basel Accords, may affect the availability of loans to businesses. An increase in capital requirements may lead to tighter credit conditions and higher debt financing costs. Furthermore, the capability of companies to raise equity capital may be influenced by capital market regulations, including securities regulations and disclosure requirements.

The European Union's regulations on issue prospectuses, for example, may increase the costs and time required to conduct a share issue, thus influencing capital structure decisions. Capital structure decisions in a given country are also influenced by the political and regulatory stability of the country. Companies in countries with a stable legal system and well-established economic policies may be more inclined to use long-term liabilities. In turn, in nations with volatile political situations, businesses may prefer to finance with equity capital to avoid the risks associated with unexpected legislative changes. Furthermore, several industries are subject to specific regulations that influence capital structure decisions. For example, the energy sector is often subject to regulations regarding infrastructure investment, which can require significant capital expenditures. Companies in this industry may therefore be more willing to use long-term debt financing to meet regulatory requirements. Regulations may also influence the perception of financial risk associated with various sources of funding. For example, debt restructuring regulations may influence companies' decisions to use debt in crisis situations. In countries where bankruptcy processes are more complex and costly, companies may be more cautious about increasing their debt levels. In summary, the impact of current regulations on capital structure decisions is intricate and diverse, contingent upon jurisdiction and industry specificity. Tax regulations, banking and market regulations, political stability, and industry-specific regulations are key factors that shape companies' decisions regarding the proportion of equity and debt. Understanding these influences is essential to effectively managing capital structures and optimising financing costs in a global context.

In the United States, the Securities and Exchange Commission (SEC) is the major capital market regulator, responsible for securities issuance, stock exchange operations, and investor protection. Furthermore, the Dodd-Frank Wall Street Reform and Consumer Protection Act, enacted after the 2008 financial crisis, had a significant impact on risk and leverage management in companies (Acharya et al., 2011). Regulations such as the Dodd-Frank Act impose capital requirements on banks, which may affect the availability of loans to businesses. Banks must maintain higher reserve capital, which may limit their ability to grant loans and thus influence companies' decisions regarding debt. Existing regulations attempt to promote transparency and financial stability, which influence capital structure decisions made by corporations. US companies are more likely to employ equity capital and use less aggressive leveraging techniques (Gompers & Lerner, 2022). Market legislation in the United States, particularly SEC regulations governing securities disclosure and issuance, may increase the cost of raising equity capital. However, a well-developed capital market and quick access to equity funding may mitigate these expenses. Simultaneously, the United States deducts interest on debt from its tax base, rendering debt an appealing source of financing. This often leads to greater debt for companies that want to take advantage of tax breaks. However, the introduction of restrictions on the deduction of interest, such as in the Tax Cuts and Jobs Act of 2017, which limited the deductibility of interest to 30% of EBITDA (and later EBIT), has reduced the attractiveness of debt.

Capital market laws in the European Union are coordinated regionally by the European Securities and Markets Authority (ESMA) and local regulatory authorities in each member state. Markets in Financial Instruments Directive II (MiFID II) and Capital Requirements Directive IV (CRD IV) are important rules that affect companies' financial markets and capital structures (European Commission, 2020a). EU regulations promote financial stability and investor protection, which encourages companies to take a more conservative approach to financing. Firms in Europe are more likely to use bank loans and corporate bonds, emphasising long-term relationships with financial institutions (La Porta et al., 1998). Moreover, the rise of green bonds and sustainable finance reflects regulatory support for sustainable development. Similar to the United States, many EU countries deduct interest from their tax bases. However, in order to minimise taxes, many countries have introduced thin capitalisation rules that limit the possibility of excessive debt. The Anti-Tax Avoidance Directive (ATAD) is an example of a regulation that introduces restrictions on the deduction of interest. EU capital markets regulations, such as MiFID II and prospectus requirements, may increase the costs of issuing shares. However, the different capital markets in different EU countries offer different equity financing opportunities for companies. The European Union is characterised by relatively high political and regulatory stability, which favours long-term financial planning. Companies can use long-term debt financing with greater confidence.

China's regulatory structure is extremely centralised. The China Securities Regulatory Commission (CSRC) and the People's Bank of China (PBoC) are the main regulators for the capital market. State policies frequently link these restrictions, influencing capital availability and financing conditions (Naughton, 2018). In China, regulations promote infrastructure development and technological innovation, leading to the widespread use of concessional bank loans and state support. Because of straightforward capital access, Chinese companies tend to maintain higher levels of financial leverage. Moreover, government initiatives promoting the development of fintech and blockchain influence capital raising and debt management strategies (Hsu et al., 2019). Like many other countries, China deducts interest on debt from its tax base, thereby encouraging the use of debt. However, Chinese tax laws are often less transparent and more variable, which may introduce additional risks. The government heavily regulates China's banking sector. The China Banking Regulatory Commission (CBIRC) sets capital requirements and credit rules that affect lending availability. Chinese banks frequently prefer to lend to large, state-owned corporations, which may affect smaller companies' decisions concerning their use of equity capital. China's economy is centrally regulated, which may lead to regulatory unpredictability. Economic policy can shift quickly based on government priorities, influencing capital structure decisions. However, substantial government control over the economy can lead to long-term stability.

Regulations have a substantial impact on capital structure decisions, and they differ by geographical region. In the United States, regulation encourages transparency and stability, resulting in a more cautious attitude towards leverage. The European Union's regulations promote a conservative approach to financing and sustainable development. Centralised regulations in China encourage rapid development and high financial leverage, whereas regulations in emerging economies aim to stabilise and attract foreign capital. A global understanding of these influences is crucial to effectively managing capital structures and making strategic financial decisions. Understanding these regulatory considerations is key to effectively managing capital structures in a global context.

3.4 Risk Management Practices Influenced by Capital Structure Choices

Capital structure decisions have a direct impact on companies' risk management practices. These choices affect the operational, financial, and strategic risks of the company. In this section, we analyse how capital structure decisions affect risk management practices. High levels of debt can limit a company's ability to invest in operations and development, increasing its operational risk. Entities should therefore maintain a balance between debt and equity to ensure adequate liquidity to finance current operations and investments (Jensen & Meckling, 1976). Equity provides greater financial flexibility than debt because it does not require regular repayments. Companies that prefer equity capital can more easily adapt to changing market conditions and take advantage of emerging investment opportunities (Graham & Harvey, 2001). High levels of corporate debt increase a company's financial leverage, which may lead to a greater risk of insolvency. Companies with higher levels of debt must manage liquidity risk to ensure they are able to repay their liabilities on time. High leverage may also result in higher financing costs, especially in an environment of rising interest rates (Myers, 1977; Modigliani & Miller, 1958).

Decisions about capital structure also affect enterprises' ownership structures. High levels of equity capital may lead to dispersion of ownership, which may weaken management's control over the company's strategic decisions. In turn, debt may increase creditors' pressure on management, limiting strategic freedom (Shleifer & Vishny, 1997). Capital structure may also influence agency problems between managers and owners. High levels of debt may act as a control mechanism, forcing managers to manage firm resources more efficiently to meet debt obligations (Jensen, 1986). Capital structure choices, therefore, have a significant impact on corporate risk management practices. Managing financial, operational, and strategic risk requires a conscious approach to the proportion of debt and equity. Enterprises must take into account capital costs, liquidity, financial flexibility, ownership structure, and control mechanisms to effectively manage risk and optimise their capital structure.

In the United States, corporations typically use ownership capital with limited leverage. This is due to strict regulations and a significant supply of funds on public markets. Companies try to maintain an adequate capital structure in order to promote financial flexibility and market responsiveness (Damodaran, 2022). US companies apply advanced risk management strategies such as diversification of their sources of financing, management of credit and operational risk, and hedging using derivatives. Furthermore, organisations implement sophisticated risk monitoring systems and scenario analysis to mitigate potential hazards (Smithson, 2013). An example of a company that uses a comprehensive approach to risk management, combining financial and operational management, is General Electric (GE). The entity uses derivatives to hedge exchange rate and interest rate risks and conducts regular scenario analyses to assess the impact of various risks on its operations (GE Annual Report, 2022).

In the European Union, companies show a more conservative approach to capital structure, often using bank loans and corporate bonds. Long-term relationships with banks and financial stability are key elements of the financial strategies of European companies (La Porta et al., 1998). European companies place significant emphasis on credit and liquidity risk management. Hedging policies, such as derivative hedging, are frequently employed by companies to maintain high capital reserves.

Additionally, compliance with sustainability and social responsibility regulations influences their risk management practices (European Commission, 2020a). Siemens AG is an example of an EU entity that applies an integrated approach to risk management. Its activities take into account both financial and operational risks. The company regularly conducts risk analyses and stress tests to assess its resistance to various economic scenarios. Siemens also employs hedging strategies, such as hedging exchange rate and interest rate risks (Siemens Annual Report, 2022).

In China, businesses frequently benefit from concessional bank loans and government support, resulting in significant levels of financial leverage. Government policy and credit availability heavily influence the capital structures of Chinese enterprises (Naughton, 2018). Chinese businesses employ a wide range of strategies for managing risks, although their approach may be less advanced than that of Western enterprises. Companies frequently use state support programmes and maintain close relationships with banks, which helps to manage liquidity risk. Companies are increasingly using modern methods like hedging using derivatives (Hsu et al., 2019). One of the largest Chinese technology conglomerates that use advanced risk management techniques is Alibaba Group. In its operations, the corporation uses hedging to protect against the risk of currency exchange rates and interest rates. The company regularly monitors its risk exposures and uses diversification strategies to minimise the impact of unfavourable market changes (Alibaba Annual Report, 2022).

In summary, companies in the United States, the European Union, and China employ distinct risk management strategies tailored to their respective local economic, regulatory, and cultural contexts. In the United States, advanced risk management and financial flexibility are crucial, while Europe places more value on stability and long-term banking connections. Preferential loans and state support contribute to high levels of financial leverage in China, although businesses are progressively adopting modern risk management practices. A comprehensive grasp of these distinctions is required for effective risk management and strategic financial decision-making.

3.5 Sustainability and ESG Factors in Capital Structure Decisions

In recent years, sustainable development and environmental, social, and governance (ESG) factors have gained importance in the context of enterprise financial management. Integrating ESG factors into capital structure decisions is becoming a key element of corporate strategies. Their implementation goal is to increase the enterprise's long-term value for stakeholders while reducing risk. Recent research on the subject has created a large body of evidence supporting the positive influence of sustainable development strategies on company financial decisions. Research has shown that companies that achieve strong ESG standards have easier access to finance. Investors see corporations that effectively handle environmental, social, and governance issues as less risky. Investors increasingly prefer to invest in such enterprises, which translates into lower costs of financing both equity and debt (Giese et al., 2019; Friede et al., 2015).

High ESG standards indicate a company's responsible approach to managing its activities in the context of sustainable development, which may include pro-ecological activities, positive social relations, and strong corporate governance. Both institutional investors, including pension and insurance funds, increasingly require that their investment portfolios comply with ESG principles. An example are green bonds, which are debt instruments intended to finance pro-ecological projects. The green bond market is growing dynamically, which proves the growing demand for sustainable investments (Climate Bonds Initiative, 2020; Flammer, 2021). Integrating ESG considerations into capital structure choices is another useful risk management method. Companies that consider ESG are better equipped to face legislative, social, and environmental changes. Green policies, careful human resource management, and strong corporate governance can help to decrease operational and financial risks (Eccles et al., 2014; Porter & Kramer, 2011). Companies with high ESG standards often achieve higher financial and operational success. Energy efficiency, waste management, CO2 reduction, and other environmental activities can result in substantial cost savings. Furthermore, positive connections with employees and local communities may improve engagement and productivity, resulting in better operational outcomes (McKinsey & Company, 2020; Harvard Business Review, 2019). Despite the obvious benefits, implementing ESG techniques presents certain problems. The initial expenditures might be considerable, and implementing sustainable practices can be expensive. Furthermore, the lack of consistent ESG reporting standards makes it difficult to compare performance across firms, thereby influencing investor decisions (Sustainability Accounting Standards Board, 2018; OECD, 2015).

Companies in the United States, the European Union, and China are incorporating sustainability and ESG principles into their financial strategies, which affect how they acquire capital, manage debt, and allocate resources. This section examines how sustainability and ESG factors influence capital structure decisions in three significant areas.

In the United States, both investors and companies are increasingly considering ESG factors in their financial decisions. Sustainable investments, including the issue of green bonds, are becoming more and more common. Enterprises attempt to meet investor expectations and legislation regulating sustainable development (Eccles et al., 2014). US companies are integrating ESG factors into their capital strategies, which often also leads to the selection of more sustainable sources of financing. Moreover, increased attention to ESG factors impacts risk management and long-term financial stability (Clark et al., 2015). In turn, some sectors, such as the renewable energy sector, can benefit from preferential financing conditions, thanks to regulations supporting the green economy (Pijourlet, 2013; Bhuiyan & Nguyen, 2019). The United States has introduced a number of laws and regulations that promote sustainable development and ESG factors. The Clean Air Act (CAA), the Energy Policy Act, and the Inflation Reduction Act (IRA) are all examples of vital legislation. The CAA is the fundamental legislative regulation that limits air pollution emissions in the United States. Since its introduction in 1963, this Act has undergone numerous amendments to adapt to evolving environmental protection requirements. The CAA regulates harmful substances and greenhouse gas emissions, such as carbon dioxide, and mandates that companies meet strict air pollution reduction targets. Established in 1972, the Clean Water Act (CWA) aims to protect US surface waterways from pollution. This legislation specifies water quality standards and requires licenses for substances emitted into the water. The CWA has significantly enhanced US water quality, benefiting both human health and the environment. The Energy Policy Act, passed in 2005, encourages energy efficiency and renewable energy sources through tax reductions and other incentives. The goal is to reduce the US dependence on fossil fuels and promote sustainable energy development. The last of the key regulations, that is, the IRA, adopted in 2022, contains a wide range of provisions aimed at reducing greenhouse gas emissions and promoting green energy. To accelerate the transition to a low-emission economy, this act introduces tax breaks for investments in renewable energy and financing for low-emission technologies. One of the leaders in sustainability and ESG fields is Apple Inc. The entity regularly issues green bonds to finance renewable energy and energy efficiency projects. Apple has also committed to achieving carbon neutrality by 2030, which influences capital structure and investment decisions (Apple, 2022).

The European Union is a global leader in encouraging sustainability and ESG integration into enterprise financial decisions. The EU is also implementing various policies as part of the European Green Deal to promote sustainable investment and finance. The entities operating within this area are increasingly issuing green bonds, investing in ESG funds, and offering other sustainable financial products. The EU is at the forefront of global ESG activities, with strict regulations and reporting standards. The EU is promoting corporate transparency and responsibility through new rules like the Corporate Sustainability Reporting Directive (CSRD) and building energy efficiency standards. The directive intends to improve the transparency and consistency of sustainability reports issued by significant

European enterprises. The CSRD replaces and broadens the scope of the previous Non-Financial Reporting Directive (NFRD), necessitating more extensive and required reporting on sustainability issues such as greenhouse gas emissions, diversity, environmental impact, and human rights. The European Union expects this directive to contribute to achieving its climate and environmental goals by promoting sustainable finance and integrating ESG into companies' business strategies. Businesses in the EU must incorporate ESG into their capital strategies, which often leads to a greater emphasis on equity financing rather than debt (Linklaters, 2024). The EU taxonomy and other regulations strive to align capital allocation with sustainable development goals. Taxonomy is the common name for the new European Union legal act, that is, Regulation (EU) 2020/852 of the European Parliament and Council of June 18, 2020, created to facilitate sustainable investment. The EU Taxonomy is a classification system that defines which economic activities can be considered environmentally sustainable. It also supports investments in sustainable projects and technologies, aiding in the shift towards a low-emission economy. The taxonomy covers six environmental objectives, including climate change mitigation, climate change adaptation, sustainable use and conservation of water and marine resources, transition to a circular economy, pollution prevention and control, and protection of biodiversity and ecosystems. By redirecting capital from environmentally harmful investments to greener alternatives, the new regulations aim to enhance environmental protection. In other words, the taxonomy does not introduce a ban on investing in activities that harm the environment but grants additional preferences for ecological solutions. Companies are required to report their ESG activities, which affects transparency and investor trust (HLEG, 2018). The European Green Deal includes a strategy to transform the EU into a climate-neutral economy by 2050. The Sustainable Finance Disclosure Regulation (SFDR), on the other hand, mandates financial market participants to disclose information about their sustainability policies. An example of a company in the EU that actively integrates ESG factors is Siemens AG, a German technology giant. The entity integrates sustainable development and ESG into its financial strategies. The company regularly issues green bonds to finance renewable energy and energy efficiency projects. Siemens has committed to achieving carbon neutrality by 2030, which influences decisions regarding capital structure and investments (Siemens, 2022).

China, as one of the world's largest generators of greenhouse gases, has recently prioritised sustainability and ESG issues. The Chinese government has initiated a number of initiatives to encourage green investment and reduce emissions (Naughton, 2018). The Environmental Protection Law, amended in 2015, governs China's environmental protection. It also imposes strong fines for pollution and requires companies to implement environmentally friendly practices. This legislation seeks to enhance the quality of the air, water, and soil while also protecting public health. In turn, the Renewable Energy Law, approved in 2006, encourages the growth of renewable energy sources like wind, solar, and biofuels. It sets incentives and other financial support mechanisms for renewable energy projects in order to minimise China's dependency on fossil fuels. The Circular Economy Promotion Law, passed in 2008, promotes recycling, material reuse, and waste reduction. These policies seek to reduce the environmental effects of economic operations while encouraging long-term growth. China launched a scheme (the National Climate Change Scheme) in 2007 to combat climate change by increasing energy efficiency and lowering greenhouse gas emissions. This strategy encompasses a variety of measures, including industrial modernisation, low-emission technology development, and green investment promotion. Companies are incorporating ESG elements into their capital plans to satisfy regulatory requirements and attract investors (Hsu et al., 2019). China Three Gorges Corporation, a Chinese energy corporation, is issuing green bonds to help fund renewable energy projects. The corporation has pledged to increase the proportion of renewable energy in its portfolio, which impacts capital structure and investment decisions (China Three Gorges, 2022).

Sustainability and ESG considerations have a substantial effect on global corporate capital structure decisions. Companies in the United States, the European Union, and China are incorporating sustainability and ESG principles into their financial strategies, which affect how they acquire capital, manage debt, and allocate resources. Companies in the United States, the European Union, and China are using best practices to meet investor expectations and requirements. In the United States, growing attention to ESG concerns affects long-term financial stability. In the EU, policies supporting sustainable development influence how businesses obtain funds and invest. In China, the growing importance of sustainability and government initiatives influence corporate capital decisions. Integrating ESG and sustainability into capital structures is not only beneficial for the environment, but it also increases transparency, investor confidence, and long-term financial stability for companies.

4 Designing a Research Framework

4.1 Defining Research Philosophy and Data Models

The development of research design should begin with the researcher's clearly stated research philosophy (Easterby-Smith et al., 2015), primarily belonging to realism, objectivism (positivism), constructivism, or pragmatism. Research philosophy is less about a decision than about the researcher's a priori existing values and attitudes, resulting in a system of assumptions and beliefs about the nature of knowledge (Saunders et al., 2016). Therefore, a researcher's lifecycle shapes a research philosophy, which typically lacks a clear definition of the nature of knowledge or science, nor does it stem from a rational decision-making process (Saunders et al., 2016).

This study's meta-theoretical basis is objectivism, which posits the existence of an observer-independent reality in the form of objective financial data. Financial accounting conventions collect and calculate these data, standardising the collection and aggregation of information. These data are numerical and structured, allowing us to objectively measure management decisions, which are social constructions by nature, given the definitions and standardisation.

In summary, this study takes a constructionist view by adopting the firm's financial data model as a mental model (Napier, 2009).The study, on the other hand, employs a positivist perspective by leveraging numerical data to generate robust assumptions about cause-and-effect relationships. According to reporting standards (Most, 1977), the existing firm data model can be considered an intersubjective model of the firm, established to inform various external stakeholders about the firm's business economics (Sunder & Yamaji, 1999). Thus, this study draws on both constructionist and positivist perspectives to provide a comprehensive understanding of firm performance.

A model represents a system of model components and defines the relationships among them (Bryman & Bell, 2011). However, business

DOI: 10.4324/9781003545194-5

administration research rarely distinguishes between the two elements of the scientific method. While a theory consists of a system of scientifically substantiated statements to explain certain facts or phenomena and underlying laws, a model is an abstract, simplified representation of the essential influencing factors of a process or the elements of a system (Burke, 2002).

At a fundamental level, it is possible to convert a theory into a model, but the reverse is not necessarily true (Bryman & Bell, 2011). Like a theory, a model serves to structure relevant knowledge about a subject area into an orderly format, resulting in a conceptualisation of the observed reality. Both theory and modelling achieve this by establishing a system of relationships.

However, while a theory takes shape through the system of linguistic descriptions of the interaction of system elements and cause-and-effect relationships, a model represents the relationships through visualisations, usually in the form of graphic representation for heuristic, content-based models or through mathematical calculations for formal models (Zikmund et al., 2009).

Consequently, a model is a simplified representation of a subject area. Helfrich (2016) states that the process of building a model involves the following requirements:

- The reduction of the subject area's complexity leads to a simplified representation of reality.
- The definition of the relationships between the model components is crucial.

We distinguish two types in principle: (1) heuristic models and (2) formal models.

- Heuristic models as well as heuristic theories refer to a particular observed area of reality, focusing on the inherent structure of the observed segment of reality. Heuristic models are either descriptive or functional. They describe a structure of functional relationships.
- Formal models are quantitative models. They describe a system of components by their formal, quantitative relationships.

Formal models are expressed as an objective, mathematical function that represents the variable to be optimised in terms of specific independent variables (input variables). Business research and economics primarily use formal models to enhance economic activities, processes, and outcomes, as well as forecast economic trends. Formal models help to maximise or minimise target indicators.

The system of external financial reporting, which includes the income statement, balance sheet, and cash flow statement, can be interpreted as a formal financial model of the firm. This "accounting model of the firm" (Bruner et al., 1998) stems from the requirements of shareholders, as well as financial regulations and legislation that define its components and collect firm-specific data for these components (Wahlen et al., 2016). As a result, some researchers consider the firm's financial reporting model to be independent and "a rational abstraction of the firm's economic and decision-making processes" (Zambon, 2013).

In conclusion, this study adopts both objectivism and constructivism as its research philosophy. The constructivist view of a firm is based on its accounting model. This allows us to use financial analysis as the primary theory, explaining what financial indicators measure and how to interpret evidence from data analysis of individual companies or cause-and-effect models derived from data analysis of a sample of companies.

This study is based on the observation that changes in accounting data make all business-relevant activities visible. All business-relevant qualitative activities lead to transactions recorded in the accounting system sooner or later and are – in the case of limited companies and listed companies – aggregated and presented in external financial reporting.

Another thing that has helped bring accounting and valuation rules together across countries and regions is the ongoing process of international standardisation and the use of clearer definitions, such as in the Generally Accepted Accounting Principles (GAAP) and International Financial Reporting Standards (IFRS) (Zimmermann & Werner, 2013). This standardisation has led to the creation of highly objective and comparable financial reporting data. Consequently, researchers and practitioners are able to compare financial data across different firms and industries, as well as over time, with greater accuracy and reliability.

The financial model of the firm consists of three main components, namely the income statement, balance sheet, and cash flow statement, as defined by reporting standards (Most, 1977). The primary purpose of establishing this model was to provide data and information to the external stakeholders of the firm regarding its business economics, as noted by Sunder and Yamaji (1999). It hereby ensures that there is a high level of standardisation in the presentation and documentation of financial data.

Some researchers note that the financial reporting data model represents a specific model of the firm, which also implies another specific theory of the firm, as the financial model is "*a rational abstraction of the firm's economic and decision-making processes*" (Zambon, 2013). According to new institutional economics, a firm is the result of contracts and business decisions made by managers, employees, stockholders, suppliers, and customers.

To observe management activities and their effect on firm performance, the collection of intentions, attitudes, and other personal characteristics as preferred in qualitative research is not necessary: "Success is based on results, not motivation" (Alchian, 1950). As a result, this study focuses primarily on measurable managerial results, which become apparent in changes in financial data, and does not examine management decisions. Only the supplementary case studies use qualitative data to triangulate the results of the statistical data analysis.

Three components make up the firm's financial model, each providing different classes of accounting indicators: The balance sheet provides stock variables, while the income statement and cash flow statement provide flow variables (Sunder & Yamaji, 1999). A stock variable indicates a quantity in existence at a moment in time, whereas a flow variable measures the change of an indicator over a period of time and measures the aggregated quantity (amount) of past flows of money or goods (Dwivedi, 2010):

- According to Stolowy and Lebas (2013), the income statement serves as documentation of all transactions related to the firm's activities on the level of business operations that impact the firm's success, specifically those associated with serving customers within the accounting period.
- The balance sheet and the cash flow statement provide documentation for the results of activities related to investing and financing (Stolowy & Lebas, 2013). According to Stolowy and Lebas (2013), the cash flow statement explains how the firm's activities generate cash and how operational, financing, and investing activities influence or alter the cash position.

Thus, the accounting data provide an implicit model of business activities (Stolowy & Lebas, 2013). The framework of this research views firm performance as the outcome of numerous decisions observed in the accounting data. Change rates, fluctuations in stock and flow variables, and ratios provide information on resource allocation decisions, enabling the observation of three crucial areas of management activities (McMenamin, 1999).

- Cash flows from operating activities represent the cash inflows and outflows related to the firm's core business operations, such as cash received from customers for goods and services and cash paid out to suppliers for inventory or other operating expenses.
- Cash flows from investing activities represent the cash outflows for purchasing or investing in tangible and intangible assets, such as property, plant and equipment, and intellectual property.

- Cash flows from financing activities represent the cash inflows and outflows related to the firm's financing activities, such as raising new capital through the issuance of bonds or shares, resulting in cash inflows, and repayments of debt capital, such as loans. This category also includes dividend payments to shareholders.

Business activities create transactions that are recorded in the accounting system and transformed by a regulated procedure into financial statement data. Therefore, the financial statement data are the end result of an economic activity reporting cycle that is grounded in economic activity events. Figure 4.1. illustrates the process.

Financial analysis research provides the necessary instruments to interpret these types of data. The analysis of key financial figures is a common method for the analysis of such data to assess the business performance of a company. Ratios are of particular importance for the interpretation of the raw data from the annual report (Ginter et al., 2018), such as (1) liquidity ratios, (2) profitability ratios, (3) asset ratios, and (4) capital structure.

The basis for the analysis of the most important activities in a company is formed by the data from the financial analysis (Albrecht et al., 2011). These include activities of (1) operational management, (2) financial management, and (3) investment management.

- Operating activities in the context of operations management are defined as all events involving buying inventory, manufacturing processes, and selling products and services (Albrecht et al., 2008), so that operating activities are equal to the concept of the input-output transformation of the firm. All these results are reflected in accounting data because all operating activities are associated with financial transactions, such as paying for necessary expenses and income from selling activities.
- Financing activities in the context of financial management involve raising money to finance business operations by means other than the cash flow from business operations. As such, financing activities are defined as all transactions and events whereby resources are obtained from or repaid to creditors (debt financing) and owners (equity financing) (Albrecht et al., 2008). Financing activities can be broken down

Figure 4.1 Economic Activity Reporting Cycle

Source: Ginter et al. (2018, p. 599).

into financing decisions in terms of managing equity and liabilities and managing the payout of dividends (dividend policy) in the framework of the management's shareholder policy.

- In investment management, investment activities encompass all transactions and events that involve the sale and purchase of tangible and intangible assets, including financial assets (Albrecht et al., 2008). The investment behaviour of the "average firm" typically follows market cycles, as evidenced by strong empirical evidence (e.g., Brost, 2005). Therefore, growth is largely dependent on market cycles, which justifies both the stochastic and microeconomic perspectives on firm growth. The differences in growth behaviour among firms can only be attributed to qualitative factors, such as better management, according to the MBV and RBV of the firm. This study does not aim to explain growth through the visible hand of management or the invisible hand of the market, but rather through the observation of corporate behaviour in terms of financials, including differences in growth, investment, and financing behaviour.

All three types of management activities can be subsumed under the terms business management and financial management, following the guidelines of strategic management in determining financial market policies and the product-market strategy. Each management activity leads to costs and revenues, income and expenses, and cash inflow and cash outflow, as reported in the income statement, the cash flow statement, and the balance sheet, and is measured by asset metrics, capital structure indicators, financial strength metrics (financing ratios, which serve as indicators of the capital structure), as well as performance and profitability indicators, as those shown in Table 4.1.

As mentioned, the analysis of indicators and ratios enables the analysis of management activities for company outsiders. Thus, for example, the ratio analysis aims at evaluating the effectiveness of the management activities in each of these areas. Ratio analysis involves relating the financial data to underlying business activities and indicators (Palepu et al., 2007). The main ratios for assessing operating management efficiency are (1) gross profit margin and (2) administration cost in percent of revenue (Palepu et al., 2007). The gross margin is influenced by three factors: (1) the price premium that a firm's products or services generate; (2) the efficiency of the production process and the cost efficiency of operations; and (3) the cost efficiency of procurement. The price premium a firm's products or services can command is influenced by the degree of competition and the extent to which its products are unique (Palepu et al., 2007). As a consequence, performance can be visualised in principle in relation to numerous variables that are interrelated. The principle of these relations is shown in Figure 4.2.

Table 4.1 Management activity indicators and business performance indictors (examples)

Indicator groups	*Exemplary variables*	*Description*
Firm growth	- Revenue growth - Market capitalisation growth - Net income growth	Such variables are indicators for the business success of the management's decisions and the output from firm-specific skills and knowledge in the areas of strategy, procurement, research and development, operations, and financing. Firm growth variables represent the results of all explicit or implicit decisions and actions of the organisation in interaction with market forces.
Operations efficiency	- Asset turnover - Operating margin - Cash conversion cycle	Efficiency can be defined as the difference between input and output. Such variables describe the efficiency of operations on different levels.
Investment activities	- Investments in property, plants, and equipment (PPE) - Acquisitions, net - R&D expenditures as % revenue - Investments in technology - Capital expenditures as % revenue - Intangible assets as % total assets	Such variables indicate how the firm expands and, in comparison with measures like debt issued and the debt-to-equity ratio, how the firm finances growth.
Capital efficiency (profitability)	- Working capital to total capital - Capital expenditures as % revenue - ROA - ROE - ROIC	Management is efficient when it uses the lowest amount of input to create the greatest amount of output. Capital efficiency ratios indicate the efficiency of using the difference.
Financing activities	- Financial leverage - Debt/equity - Dividend paid - Retained earnings	Such variables indicate capital structure decisions (financing decisions).

Source: Own presentation.

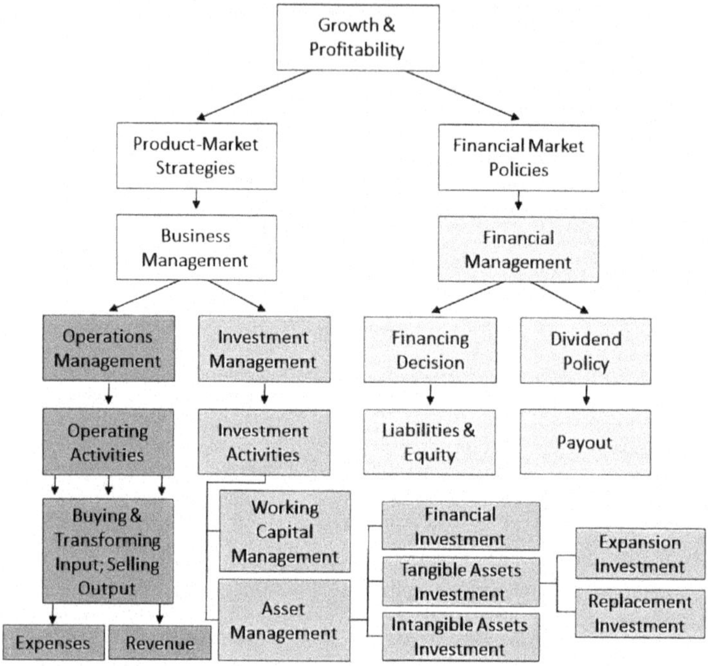

Figure 4.2 Model of management objectives, activities, and outcomes

Source: Own presentation referring to Palepu et al., 2007.

4.2 Formulating Research Questions and Hypotheses

In summary, the current state of research on capital structure and business performance indicates that empirical studies investigating the reasons for selecting a particular capital structure yield inconsistent results with regard to the rationality of financing decisions. This gap in understanding the factors contributing to the heterogeneity of capital structures among companies serves as the starting point for this research. This study aims to explore the relationship between capital structure and business performance by examining investment activities, operations activities, and financing activities. As there is relatively little research on the recursive relationship between capital structure and business performance, this approach is considered exploratory in nature (Iyoha & Umoru, 2017; Margaritis & Psillaki, 2010).

As previously mentioned in the Introduction, this study employs financial analysis research to delve into secondary data, specifically financial data from companies listed on stock exchanges. It aims to investigate the correlation between management activities, including operations and investment activities, management efficiency, and business performance, including firm growth and profitability, in relation to capital structure, in order to address the research questions posed.

1. Can business performance differences explain the capital structure choices of firms? (RQ1)
2. Can capital structure explain differences in business performance? (RQ2)

Since the discussed research areas (capital structure, firm growth, and firm performance) led to a multitude of factor models and found a multitude of different correlations between a multitude of variables, this study follows an explorative research approach. Therefore, this study does not confirm or reject an existing factor model or assume cause-and-effect relationships based on the discussed literature. Consequently, we do not develop a research model or hypotheses. Different steps of the research procedure examine both factor dimension.

4.3 Strategies for Sampling and Data Collection

This study is based exclusively on financial data from the annual financial reporting statements. The data have been gathered from GuruFocus, a financial data service provider. The research questions are answered through the explorative analysis of financial data. The sample includes listed companies headquartered in Germany. Obviously, the focus on Germany allows for the consideration of data from a leading trading economy with strong export activities and an important manufacturing sector and services sector (BMWI, 2021; Prittwitz, 2022) as well as a leading international position in knowledge-based industries, as exemplified by German companies' strongly established role in research and development (Belitz et al., 2019).

Focusing on a single country is beneficial because it eliminates potential external intervening variables, a common problem in cross-country studies (Schmitt, 2009; Havlik et al., 2012). However, it's important to note that despite the data offering a general overview of the German economy, the presence of a substantial number of medium-sized firms, known as Mittelstand in German (Mueller, 2007), may potentially exclude a significant number of economically significant firms from the sample due to their non-listing status. The selection of only companies from Germany also provides an argument for the assumption that the subjects are active within a comparable business environment regarding the tax system; they operate with the same interest rates and highly comparable regulations, such as corporate governance regulations, accounting and report regulations, and others (Schmitt, 2009, p. 123; Havlik et al., 2012). However, given the significant international activity of globally oriented German firms (Belitz et al., 2019), it is reasonable to assume that additional regulations and market characteristics unique to their specific field of business also heavily impact German firms. However, we can assume that the sample companies exhibit a higher degree of similarity in terms of issues such as tax treatment, insolvency proceedings, financial market conditions, and other similar factors than a truly internal set of companies headquartered in different countries. Consequently, regarding the capital structure, the irrelevance proposition theorem and the trade-off theory are the same for all included companies.

The observation period to be used as the database within this research spans a total of 12 years and is set to range from the year 2008 to 2019. Academics are generally interested in historical data for German stock market returns during this time period, leading to more extensive research in this area (Stehle & Schmidt, 2015). For this observation period, sufficiently complete time series of financial data are available. Unfortunately, when attempting to use earlier data from before the year 2008, the data quality was not satisfactory enough to justify the inclusion of the data. Such data are only available in the case of some companies that have a long tradition of being listed on the German stock market. For example, the data show that in the particular case of MAN SE, an industrial firm, the available data even go back for a long time until the 1970s. However, this example is an exception. Consequently, data from before the observation period cannot be included due to availability issues. Additionally, we removed the year 2020 from the final dataset for the empirical analysis because some firms had missing values.

We gathered the data in the form of panel data, also known as longitudinal data. A panel dataset is hereby characterised by having a cross-sectional as well as a time series component (Wooldridge, 2013). The total panel includes financial data from 361 different German-listed firms[1] for which a total of 4,229 firm years are available. However, it is important to note that the availability of firm-year data does not guarantee the availability of all variables for every firm during the time period, as some firms still lack data from the financial service provider.

Additionally, the inclusion or delisting of some stocks in the data may introduce a survivorship bias. This does potentially cause a distortion of statistics drawn from such data, as studies referring to other indices have shown (Davis, 2015). However, the data observation reveals a relatively small number of delisted firms, suggesting a minimal delisting bias in the

Table 4.2 Overview of firm data

Years with firm data in sample	*Included firms per year*	*% of dataset*
2008	361	8.5
2009	356	8.4
2010	358	8.5
2011	357	8.4
2012	355	8.4
2013	353	8.3
2014	353	8.3
2015	351	8.3
2016	353	8.3
2017	348	8.2
2018	344	8.1
2019	341	8.1
Total	-	**100.0**

Source: Own presentation.

data. Table 8 presents an overview of firm data, revealing that the delisting of firms has occurred within the last couple of years.

The sample delisting effect is consistent with the general market trend of decreasing numbers of listed companies, which has been observed not only in Germany but also in the United Kingdom and the United States (Katsamitros, 2019). As such, it must not necessarily impact the analysis of capital structure and its relation to business performance, and vice versa, particularly because delisting is relatively rare, as is evidenced by Table 4.2.

4.4 Addressing Outliers for Robust Analysis

A challenge in the analysis of financial data is the presence of outliers in the form of extreme values in the dataset. When these outliers are generally interpreted as noise rather than valuable information, it is recommended to remove this subgroup of data from the final dataset used for the research question analysis. Retaining such data could potentially lead to misinterpreted analysis results and false conclusions. The literature on empirical finance mentions two primary methods for resolving these issues. The methods described below (Ang, 2021) include winsorisation and truncation.

- Winsorisation: This denotes replacement of the values that are present above or below a certain threshold in the form of a percentile, like at the level of 0.5%, with the value at this cut-off point.[2]
- Truncation: Unlike the winsorising procedure, truncation eliminates data outside the percentiles that the researcher defines as outliers.

In general, we can assert that there is no established guideline for applying these data manipulation techniques or for selecting winsorisation or truncation in specific scenarios. Based on the analysis's demands, we determine the best choice. Additionally, we should scrutinise the choice of a specific method more thoroughly if it significantly alters the outcomes, thereby influencing the results (Ang, 2021). Additionally, it is possible to select the cut-off points for winsorisation (or truncation) at a different level than the 0.5% level previously mentioned. Other authors, such as Braun et al. (2017) and Habib et al. (2013), perform winsorisation using 1% for the percentiles and in the context of ratios calculated from financial statements, such as performance ratios. This is comparable to the method in this monograph, where winsorisation was applied using a 1% percentile.

4.5 Overview of Key Elements in the Study

The basic financial data that have been gathered from the financial data provider GuruFocus were used to derive suitable variables regarding capital structure and performance. Regarding performance, operational, investment management, and other indicators have been used. The final set of data includes a total of 13 variables, which are shown in Table 4.3.

In order to analyse the different groups that exist within the dataset, relevant subsets of the total data were defined. The criteria for the definition of the subsets were based on differences in growth behaviour (high growth versus low growth), company size, and company type (i.e., industry). Specifically, the following subsets have been constructed:

1. *Revenue growth*: two subsets based on the median value, with a group having lower and higher growth, respectively;
2. *Profitability growth*: similar to revenue growth, but both groups are distinguished using profitability growth;
3. *Size*: two groups with the log of total assets [1] as a distinguishing factor and the median used for group definition;
4. *Company type*: Three subsets of the data have been defined, which represent the three most frequent industries in the data: industrials, technology, and consumer cyclical. These can be mentioned as typical for representing the German market according to the stock market data.

4.6 Methods for Data Interpretation and Insight Generation

This chapter's final section will explain the methodological approach to data analysis. These include bivariate analysis and regression analysis. We also used an artificial neural network to analyse the data, and we will describe it later. We will conclude with a discussion about group differentiation. The

Table 4.3 Overview of variables

Variable	*Code*	*Calculation/definition*
Capital structure variables		
Debt ratio	DE	Ratio of debt to total assets
Interest coverage ratio (EBIT/interest expense)	EI	EBIT divided by interest expense
Long-term debt/total debt	LTD	Long-term debt divided by total assets
Operational management indicators for performance		
Operating margin	OM	Ratio of operating income divided by revenue (net sales)
Asset turnover	AT	Sales divided by total assets
ROE	ROE	Return on a firm's equity (tangible equity)
YoY revenue growth	REV	Yearly growth in revenues
YoY profit growth	PRO	Yearly growth of net income
Investment management indicators for performance		
ROIC	ROIC	Return on invested capital[3]
CAPEX/total assets	CAP	Total capital expenditures divided by total assets
ROA	ROA	Return on total assets
Other indicators for performance		
Price-to-book ratio	PB	Ratio of price to book value
Price-to-earnings ratio	PE	Price divided by earnings

Source: Own presentation

first subsection below provides an overview of the methods. We perform the data analysis in several distinct steps. Most of the methods applied can be considered independent of each other. However, the bivariate analysis, which is the first step in the analysis, also serves to exclude specific variables from subsequent analyses, such as regressions. Table 4.4. illustrates the step-by-step execution of the analytical procedure.

Bivariate analysis is an analysis between two single variables, such as in a simple linear regression model, involving only variables (Wooldridge, 2013). Similarly, the correlation coefficient between two variables provides another type of bivariate analysis. In this monograph, the Pearson correlation coefficient was used for every possible dichotomous combination of variables, as depicted in Table 9. The Pearson correlation coefficient is not dependent on the scale of measurement and is also independent of sample size. It is defined to range between +1.00 and -1.00, which indicates a perfect positive or negative correlation, respectively. Values for the Pearson correlation coefficient of 0.00 point to the conclusion that no relationship between variables exists (Tabachnick & Fidell, 2013).

Table 4.4 Statistical analysis procedure

Step/method	*Sample and variables*	*Methods and statistical tests*
Step 1: Bivariate analysis	Total sample	Calculation of bivariate correlations between variables; calculation of variance inflation factor
Step 2: Regression analysis	Total sample Selected samples distinguished by differences in revenue growth, profit growth, size, and company type	Panel regression analysis; stepwise forward regression, regression with fixed and random effects Hausman test
Step 3: Artificial neural network (ANN) analysis	Same as in step 2	Determination of predictive capabilities of variables with using a linear regression model in the ANN environment
Group comparison	Comparison of selected subgroups as defined in step 2 regarding growth in revenue and in profitability as well as regarding size and industry (three top industries in Germany) Evaluation of top and bottom halves of the dataset for each group	Interpretation of differences of results from preceding analysis regarding the sub-datasets (groups) Application of t-test for mean value differences of important variables

Source: Own presentation

While bivariate correlations have their place in the analysis, they also have drawbacks. For example, bivariate correlations cannot reveal whether there are potential factors within the data that can serve as super-variables (Tabachnick & Fidell, 2013). Also, the analysis of the correlations between input variables can give the researcher valuable information on potentially existing problems in the calculational model. As such, the interpretation of the correlation coefficients serves as a type of data reduction method as well. Data reduction is applied in multivariate statistics as a way of summarising information from multiple variables into a reduced form. This can be performed via different techniques, for example, factor analysis (Zikmund et al., 2009). In this thesis, factor analysis was not applied. That is because the total number of variables is considered to be relatively low, so bivariate correlations between variables will be sufficient to detect considerable relations in the data. This is helpful in the case of analytical techniques such as linear regression, whereas methods involving an artificial network do not necessarily suffer from highly correlated input variables (Pao, 2008).

In addition to the analysis of bivariate correlations between variables, the variance inflation factor (VIF) and tolerance (TOL) were also calculated for controlling multicollinearity effects among regression predictors. Collinearity exists if there are variables that constitute nearly perfect linear combinations, while multicollinearity means that multiple variables show such behaviour (Belsley et al., 1980). Both indicators, VIF and TOL, indicate that there is some level of collinearity. They can therefore be used for the evaluation of the quality of the model used such as the regression models:

- The VIF is a measure of the extent to which multicollinearity effects increase variance (Hair et al., 2014). Generally, there is no widely accepted threshold for the VIF, with some scholars proposing that multicollinearity is not significant if the VIF is less than 10 (Mertler & Reinhart, 2017), while others advocate for a VIF below 3 (Hair et al., 2014). A VIF value of 1 indicates the complete absence of any collinearity effects (Hair et al., 2014). Most scholars consider a variance inflation factor of less than 5 to indicate negative multicollinearity (Pedhazur, 1997; Bonate, 2011).
- The tolerance is the reciprocal of the VIF and indicates the proportion of a predictor's variance that is explained by other predictors included in the regression model. A tolerance of 0, which is equivalent to a VIF of 1, indicates no multicollinearity, meaning that the standard error of the regression model is not affected. A tolerance of 0.25, on the other hand, implies high multicollinearity, as 75% of the predictor's variance can be explained by another predictor in the regression model (Hair et al., 2014). As VIF = 1/TOL, a TOL of 0.25 is equivalent to a VIF of 4 (1/0.25 = 4).
- Some researchers recommend a TOL > 0.8, which is equivalent to a VIF of > 1.25 (1/0.8 = 1.25) to select the final model or assess the quality of a regression model (e.g., Scheld, 2013). Following this recommendation, this research applies a very strict cut-off threshold for the assessment of a regression model or the selection of the final regression model among several models.

The measurement of VIF and TOL allows to control multicollinearity. In the case that several variables should be included or are entered in the regression model because it is necessary for theoretical reasons, the robustness of a model can be assessed by referring to these metrics (Schneider, 2010). In the case of forward selection of the independent variables, a limit value is to be set accordingly, limited by a cut-off point to the number of possible regression models.

Moreover, the problem of outliers should be discussed. It is generally assumed that the OLS-based regression analysis using small samples is sensitive to outliers (Wooldridge, 2013). Among a small sample, only a single outlier may produce exceptionally low or high regression coefficients. In larger samples, however, the normality assumption loses its significance, as the coefficients become increasingly independent of the distribution of the residuals according to the central limit theorem (Backhaus et al., 2018). Then, only extreme outliers can distort the regression coefficients (Cleves et al., 2010). According to Backhaus et al. (2018) and Wooldridge (2013), reality is characterised by outliers, whereas a bell curve distribution of observed values is the exception. Consequently, the normal distribution assumption is principally violated (Baltes-Götz, 2018). Therefore, the central limit theorem states that the observations for a variable can also be considered as normally distributed if the number of observations is sufficiently large (Wooldridge, 2013).

Moreover, the multiple linear regression can be considered sufficiently robust against violations of the normal distribution assumption. According to the central limit theorem, a normal distribution can be assumed even in very small samples if the mean and median are very similar (Treyer, 2003). Consequently, this research observes the robustness of the regression analysis, mainly by comparing the median and the mean for each variable in discussing the quality of a regression model. Also, issues regarding the impact of outliers are potentially mitigated due to the winsorisation of variables as well.

Generally, a linear regression model describes the proposed or assumed linear relationship between a dependent and an independent variable (Wei, 2019). In the case of a linear relationship between a single independent variable, the model can be referred to as a simple linear regression model. In linear regression, the dependent variable is also called the explained variable, while the independent variable can be called the explanatory variable, regressor, or predictor variable (Wooldridge, 2013). Regression analysis is, therefore, used as a technique for examining quantitative relationships between the predictor variable and the predicted variable.

In the case of multiple independent variables within a regression model, the model forms a multiple regression analysis. Here, the dependent variable is predicted with a set of independent variables. Due to its flexibility and improved ability for estimating parameters, the multiple regression methodology is a commonly used model in the empirical literature within economics or social science (Wooldridge, 2013). Multivariate statistical methods, therefore, provide an extension to bivariate statistics, which are also mentioned as univariate statistics. Generally, relationships of bivariate nature are special cases of multivariate statistics (Tabachnick & Fidell, 2013).

Due to the large number of variables, the stepwise forward regression method was applied first in order to obtain a relevant set of predictors, which are later used for fixed- and random-effects regression. The stepwise forward regression method is performed by gradually adding predictor variables in a stepwise manner to the regression equation based on their explanatory power. The explanatory power is hereby measured by the R^2 measure of the regression model. Basically, the stepwise procedure works such that not all variables are introduced simultaneously into the regression model but in a stepwise procedure (Holtmann, 2010).

In the stepwise forward regression model, the first independent variable needs to be mentioned as the most important variable, as this variable is able to best explain[4] the variance of the dependent variable. The independent variable, therefore, shows the highest correlation with the dependent variable. Subsequently, other variables are added to the original regression model, each able to explain an additional portion of the variance. Specifically, given that the first variable is the best for explaining the variance of the dependent variable, the second independent variable is useful for explaining most of the remaining variance in the model. Therefore, with the addition of independent variables to the stepwise forward regression model, the regression equation is changing accordingly (Holtmann, 2010). Generally, stepwise regression can also be regarded as a type of data mining as well, as it automates the careful selection of variables for inclusion in a model through its algorithm (Wooldridge, 2013).

In the context of evaluating the capital structure variables DE and EI on the basis of the performance variables, it is either DE or EI, while the predictor variables are OM, AT, ROE, REV, PRO, CAP, PB, or PE. Similarly, the analysis of the recursive relationship necessitates a change of independent and dependent variables. Given the results of the stepwise regression models, some of the models may occasionally be skipped from the final regression model.

The regression approach can nevertheless be stated as a panel regression, using a cross-sectional dimension with the time dimension measured in years and the respective firms stated as. The time period conforms to the reporting periods of the firms in the dataset. Mathematically, the regression equation can be described as follows:

$$y_{i,t} = a + bX_{i,t} + u_{i,t}$$

with

$$i = \frac{1}{4}, 361$$

and $.t = 1, \frac{1}{4}, 12$

In the regression equation, α is the constant, while $X_{i,t}$ refers to the vector of performance or capital structure variables, depending on whether the direct or the recursive relationship is being assessed. The symbol β depicts the vector of parameters for the independent variable vector. The error term $u_{i,t}$ can be depicted as the sum of the time ας and firm-specific ας effects plus an error term $\varepsilon_{i,t}$:

$$u_{i,t} = \mu_i + \mu_t + \varepsilon_{i,t}$$

Examples of unobserved firm-specific effects in the regression can include issues like managerial motivation or risk behaviour, whereas unobserved time-specific effects can refer to differences in macroeconomic variables, for example, in relation to the term structure of interest rates or inflation (Chen, 2004; Hackbarth, 2008). As a result, firm-specific effects can imply the existence of agency issues, which can potentially lead to incentives that are detrimental to the interests of shareholders of the firm (Jensen & Meckling, 1976). An example of this is the issue of underinvestment, which is based on conflicts between holders of equity and debt (Myers, 1977). However, unobservable firm-specific effects do not show the sheer existence of such problems but point to the existence of differences between firms.

In order to determine whether the fixed-effects or the random-effects regression model is more useful, the Hausman test is used. This test is based on the null hypothesis of repressors being uncorrelated and fixed effects being unobservable. The significance of the Hausman test will lead to a rejection of the null hypothesis, making the fixed-effects model more suitable for interpretation. Otherwise, if the null hypothesis cannot be rejected, random effects should be used (Chen, 2004). However, in practice, the failure to reject the null hypothesis in the Hausman test can simply imply that there is not much difference between fixed- and random-effects regression (Wooldridge, 2013).

Group Comparison Analysis

The computations methodologically described so far will be applied to the entire dataset of listed firms in Germany. However, they will also be applied to selected subsets of the data with the aim of finding group differences based on certain criteria. Given the results from the literature review, it is obvious that particular groups of firms could potentially exhibit different characteristics, making it worthwhile to investigate the relationship between performance and capital structure based on group distinctions. The same can be stated for the recursive relationship as well. For the purpose of the analysis, group distinctions referring to company types (or industries), growth characteristics, and size have been defined. These will be explained in more detail in the following. Also, the issue of ownership structure as a criterion for group distinction is discussed.

A central element in the analysis is the distinction between different groups that have rather homogeneous attributes or for which such attributes can be assumed. For example, performance issues are typically benchmarked and evaluated by financial analysts in comparison to firms in the same sector (Vernimmen, 2018), so group selection based on sectors appears to be worthwhile. Sector distinctions for the purpose of group definitions are used in academic studies on capital structure and performance as well, for example, for data on listed firms (Margaritis & Psillaki, 2010; Salim & Yadav, 2012). However, in order to derive meaningful results for a sector-based group analysis, a sufficient number of firms from each sector needs to be included in the analysis.

Consequently, a suitable set of homogeneous firms needs to be selected based on the firm data for the listed firms in Germany. This was performed based on the most frequent industry classification found in the data. Also, in order to have enough firm data for each group, a suitable selection of these clusters is required as well. Finally, this led to the use of data from three subsets: industrials, technology, and consumer cyclical. These can be considered highly relevant in the characterisation of the German market.

Size is used as another criterion to distinguish different subgroups as well. This indicator is also discussed in the literature. While some authors do not state that size is relevant in determining the capital structure, others point out differences. For example, Strebulaev (2007) states that large firms are simply a scaled version of smaller firms. Therefore, size does not have an impact on target leverage ratios. However, other authors assert such a relationship, claiming that differences exist between smaller firms and larger firms, that is, because of their unique financing options as a result of size differences (Frank & Goyal, 2015).

Whether there are differences in financing options among listed firms of different sizes may be subject to discussion. However, it was decided that size would be used as another criterion for group distinction as well. Therefore, two groups were defined, separating firms into low and high sizes. This is based on the log of total assets as derived from the financial statements. Similarly, for revenue and profitability growth, the median was used as the cut-off point for group distinction.

In addition to the sectors that can be used to distinguish between different groups of firms in the data, there are other factors available for a useful distinction. For example, in the study of Margaritis and Psillaki (2010), firms are distinguished in terms of growth opportunities as well as ownership structure. Whereas growth is regarded as useful to the analysis in this thesis, ownership is of potentially less relevance.

Although ownership, especially regarding the role of family firms, has been found to be relevant to explaining distinctions in structural considerations of balance sheet ratios (Lozano & Durán, 2017; Maury, 2006), it can be argued that this criterion is less relevant for this research because the data sample consists entirely of publicly traded firms. Therefore, it should not be considered further for the empirical analysis.

The analysis of group differences is approached in either of two different ways. First, an analysis like regression analysis is conducted with respect to subsets of the total data, employing the same methodology as described in the preceding paragraph. Second, group differences for selected variables are evaluated in order to identify distinctions. To examine such group differences, the t-test is applied. The t-test is a statistical method that can be used to compare the means of different groups within a sample or between a sample and a larger population. There are two types of t-tests: (1) one-sample t-test and (2) two-sample t-test. The one-sample t-test is used to determine whether a sample is representative of a population by comparing the mean of the sample to a known population mean. The two-sample t-test, on the other hand, compares the means of two different samples or groups from the same population or sample (Sirkin, 2006).

The t-test assumes that samples from the same total population or groups from the same sample are characterised by the same standard deviation. Consequently, the t-test results indicate the level of difference between the mean values of different groups or between a sample and the total population (Sirkin, 2006) by measuring the statistical significance of the differences indicated by the p-value (Sirkin, 2006). This research considers a difference at the usual level of $p < 0.05$ as significant.

The reliability of the t-test does not depend solely on the normal distribution assumption of the variable. When the group sizes are approximately equal, the t-test remains reliable, even in the case of an extreme unequal distribution (Wenzelburger et al., 2014; Bortz & Schuster, 2010). Therefore, testing for a normal distribution of the data is not necessary.

Artificial Neural Network Analysis

Another methodology that was applied for analysis was artificial neural network analysis. This type of analysis is, in principle, a type of non-parametric analysis technique that has become prominent in the last couple of years. Originating from biological phenomena, artificial neural networks are, in principle, similar to nerve cells. Within physiology, this analysis technique has been employed through engineering and for answering questions in business and finance (Campbell et al., 1997). Generally, neural networks belong to the realm of artificial intelligence, where computer algorithms are used for processing information, similar to the way humans process and learn (Zikmund et al., 2009).

By employing an artificial neural network model (ANN), it becomes theoretically possible to increase the accuracy of predictions significantly, for example, when applied to the prediction of capital structure on the basis of its respective determinants (Pao, 2008). As such, the modelling of capital structure themes is expected to improve in terms of accuracy and quality of prediction when compared with more traditional forms of quantitative methods like regression analysis. The improvement in the ability to predict capital structure parameters by employing ANNs can be mentioned as similar to results from other fields in economics and business research. Here, the application of artificial neural network analysis has proven to be able to produce more accurate results in forecasting parameters as well, including economic parameters (Kordanuli et al., 2017).

The ANN is a model that generally mimics the structure as well as the function of the human brain. As such, it is part of what is described as deep learning, which is part of the family of machine learning methods. There are several types of artificial neural networks in existence, such as the multilayer perceptron, the convolutional neural network, or deep belief networks (Wei, 2019, p. 21).

ANN models have been researched for many decades with the aim of achieving performance comparable to human-like performance, for example, in image or speech recognition. Methodologies for ANN can differ in terms of their number of layers or other computational elements (Lippmann, 1987). Also, in accounting or financial market research, ANN models can be fruitfully applied, for example, due to the fact that these models are less prone to being distorted because of the existence of outliers in the data. Generally, different types of ANN are available for use in such research (Abdou et al., 2012).

Notes

1 To ensure comparability in the sample, we have excluded a total of 44 firms from the financial sector.
2 This implies that the example replaces the values above 99.5 percent with the 99.5% level measurement. Similarly, we replace values below 0.5% with the measured value at the 0.5% level.
3 The definition of ROIC is: Return on Invested Capital (ROIC) = (EBIT – Adjusted Taxes) / (Book Value of Debt + Book Value of Equity – Cash), according to GuruFocus who provides the ROIC value.
4 It can be mentioned that the best explanation is always considered within the context of the model itself. That means that the best variable for explaining the variance is considered the best option available within the modelling context. Therefore, it cannot be stated that variables outside the model may be able to provide more of the variance.

5 Empirical Analysis for Strategic Decision-Making

5.1 Insights from Descriptive Statistics

In this section, a descriptive evaluation of the data will be provided. This includes selected aspects of the raw data but mainly relevant statistics on the variables that were calculated to serve as inputs to the empirical analysis. As already stated in the last chapter in the context of sampling and data gathering, a total of 361 different firms that are listed and headquartered in Germany have initially been gathered. For these firms, a total of 4,229 firm years are included in the dataset. The time period of the data ranges over a 12-year period, starting from the year 2008 to the end of the year 2019. It must be noted that there are some missing data for particular firm years, a topic that will be addressed further below.

Similar to other studies (e.g., Frank & Goyal, 2009; Gropp & Heider, 2008), financial service providers are excluded from the analysis. This was performed in order to ensure a sufficient level of comparability across the typical ratios used in the analysis. However, this does not mean that financial institutions like banks are not relevant to the topic, but simply that these firms belong to a particular type of industry that requires a narrower industry perspective directed solely at financial sector firms. There is academic research available that covers this topic, which is directly geared towards an analysis of such firms (e.g., Berger, 1995; Berger & Bonaccorsi di Patti, 2006; Tarek Al-Kayed et al., 2014). Due to the exclusion of firms from the financial sector, a total of 43 companies were excluded from the original data.

The first descriptive step in the analysis was the analysis of the industries. Here, an overview of the industry classification was performed based on the number of firm years in the sample. The results are shown in Table 11. The distinction of the industry is hereby to be mentioned as potentially relevant in the context of the thesis because managerial ability to design capital structure is found in empirical studies to be dependent on the industry type, especially regarding debt financing, which, again, largely depends on asset structure and profitability of firms (Börner

DOI: 10.4324/9781003545194-6

et al., 2010; Hall et al., 2000). Studies even use industry-adjusted levels for metrics like performance or cash flow (Lamont, 1997).

Regarding the industry classification, the data in Table 5.1. provide a mirror on the structure of the German economy, with its main focus being set on the service sectors but also with a relatively high percentage of industrial firms in existence that contribute to economic activity as well (BMWI, 2021).

Summary statistics for the variables, as defined in the preceding chapter, were also calculated. The results are shown in Table 5.2:

Table 5.1 Overview of the industry classification of the firms in the sample (by firm years)

Industry	*N*	*%*
Industrials	958	22.7
Technology	823	19.5
Consumer cyclical	546	12.9
Healthcare	462	10.9
Communication services	391	9.2
Real estate	362	8.6
Basic materials	283	6.7
Consumer defensive	192	4.5
Utilities	154	3.6
Energy	58	1.4
Total	4,229	100.0

Source: Own presentation.

Table 5.2 Descriptive statistics for variables

Variable	*Label*	*n*	*mean*	*sd*	*median*	*min*	*max*
Debt ratio	DE	4138	0.16	0.18	0.10	0.00	0.73
EBIT/interest expense	EI	3738	20.42	106.87	3.68	-245.70	826.27
Long-term debt/ total debt	LTD	3789	0.19	0.32	0.01	0.00	1.00
Operating margin	OM	4122	0.02	0.38	0.05	-2.30	1.00
Asset turnover	AT	4141	0.62	0.63	0.43	0.00	3.17
ROE	ROE	4090	0.08	0.49	0.08	-2.36	2.29
YoY revenue growth	REV	3322	12.80	63.50	0.03	-1.00	455.08
YoY profit growth	PRO	3652	3.57	25.83	-0.14	-23.42	224.96
ROIC	ROIC	4140	0.02	0.26	0.04	-1.56	0.72
CAPEX/total assets	CAP	3790	4.41	17.45	0.02	0.00	116.79
ROA	ROA	4141	0.74	14.78	2.88	-74.31	38.18
Price-to-book ratio	PB	4136	2.21	2.45	1.51	0.00	14.67
Price-to-earnings ratio	PE	4132	17.55	31.04	10.34	0.00	211.19

Source: Own presentation.

5.2 Delving into Bivariate Analysis

For the bivariate analysis, correlation analysis and the calculation of the variance inflation factor and the tolerance were performed in order to detect and eliminate potential highly correlated variables for further analysis. The results are shown in the paragraphs below.

Correlation Analysis

The correlation analysis shows that for the majority of the variables, there is little evidence for a linear bivariate relationship, as most correlation coefficients circle around zero. This is particularly evident for the capital structure variables in comparison to the performance variables. However, LTD shows a high correlation with DE, which is plausible, as an increased use of debt may be aligned with a higher share of long-term debt use as well. In addition, there are cases where comparable variables of performance show a relatively strong positive relationship, for example, ROE and ROA, or even ROIC as well. Return ratios also show a high correlation with OM.

In alignment with the suggestion by Abdou, Pointon, et al. (2012), variables with a high correlation have to be skipped when performing regression model calculations. The author proposes the elimination of highly correlated variables if the correlation coefficient is higher than 0.30. As a result, the variables LTD, ROIC, and ROA were dropped from further calculations because of the likelihood of the multicollinearity that these variables may cause.

Variance Inflation Factor and Tolerance

To further evaluate the issue of multicollinearity of the variables, the variance inflation factor (VIF) was also calculated. The results of the VIF calculation can hereby provide valuable insights concerning the task of identifying variables that need to be excluded from the analysis.

In order to calculate the VIF, the specification of a regression model is first required. For the purpose of this thesis, that implies the specification of several multiple regression models. First, there are two models for the specification of the performance variables as independent variables, with the capital structure variables DE and EI serving as the dependent variables. Second, the regression models use each of the performance variables as a dependent variable, with the capital structure variables serving as the independent variables, respectively.

The model VIF values were calculated, and the results are shown in Tables 5.4 and 5.5, respectively:

Table 5.3 Correlation matrix for variables

	DE	*EI*	*LTD*	*OM*	*AT*	*ROE*	*REV*	*PRO*	*ROIC*	*CAP*	*ROA*	*PB*	*PE*
DE	1.00	-0.13	0.44	0.07	-0.03	-0.01	-0.04	0.03	-0.04	0.04	-0.05	-0.02	-0.01
EI	-0.13	1.00	-0.08	0.15	0.08	0.16	0.01	0.00	0.32	-0.01	0.32	0.12	0.06
LTD	0.44	-0.08	1.00	0.11	-0.05	0.06	0.10	0.08	0.03	0.32	0.05	-0.04	0.00
OM	0.07	0.15	0.11	1.00	0.04	0.27	0.03	0.02	0.44	0.06	0.45	-0.03	0.07
AT	-0.03	0.08	-0.05	0.04	1.00	0.09	0.03	0.00	0.13	0.06	0.11	0.15	0.06
ROE	-0.01	0.16	0.06	0.27	0.09	1.00	0.02	0.04	0.38	0.05	0.49	0.02	0.06
REV	-0.04	0.01	0.10	0.03	0.03	0.02	1.00	0.00	0.03	0.11	0.03	0.01	0.00
PRO	0.03	0.00	0.08	0.02	0.00	0.04	0.00	1.00	0.01	0.00	0.02	-0.01	0.01
ROIC	-0.04	0.32	0.03	0.44	0.13	0.38	0.03	0.01	1.00	0.06	0.73	0.06	0.09
CAP	0.04	-0.01	0.32	0.06	0.06	0.05	0.11	0.00	0.06	1.00	0.07	0.02	0.04
ROA	-0.05	0.32	0.05	0.45	0.11	0.49	0.03	0.02	0.73	0.07	1.00	0.04	0.12
PB	-0.02	0.12	-0.04	-0.03	0.15	0.02	0.01	-0.01	0.06	0.02	0.04	1.00	0.15
PE	-0.01	0.06	0.00	0.07	0.06	0.06	0.00	0.01	0.09	0.04	0.12	0.15	1.00

Source: Own presentation.

Table 5.4 VIF values (regression with performance variables as independent variables)

	OM	*AT*	*ROE*	*REV*	*PRO*	*CAP*	*PB*	*PE*
DE	1.093	1.032	1.092	1.013	1.002	1.018	1.040	1.028
EI	1.101	1.031	1.102	1.013	1.003	1.018	1.042	1.027

Source: Own presentation

Table 5.5 VIF values (regression with capital structure variables as independent variables)

	DE	*EI*
OM	1.018	1.018
AT	1.018	1.018
ROE	1.019	1.019
REV	1.025	1.025
PRO	1.021	1.021
CAP	1.021	1.021
PB	1.018	1.018
PE	1.019	1.019

Source: Own presentation.

Table 5.6 TOL values (regression with performance variables as independent variables)

	OM	*AT*	*ROE*	*REV*	*PRO*	*CAP*	*PB*	*PE*
DE	0.914	0.968	0.915	0.987	0.997	0.982	0.961	0.972
EI	0.908	0.970	0.907	0.987	0.997	0.982	0.959	0.974

Source: Own presentation

The VIF results show relatively small values of close to 1. That implies that multicollinearity is not deemed to be an issue in the analysis, as this result implies nearly an absence of collinearity effects between predictors. Consequently, no further elimination of variables was performed on the basis of the VIF values as indicated in the literature, given the high VIF values for the data (Abdou, Pointon, et al., 2012; Pao, 2008). Despite the useful results from the calculation of the VIF, which imply that multicollinearity is not an issue, the values for tolerance (TOL) were calculated as well. These are shown in Tables 16 and 17, respectively.

As expected, the results for TOL imply, like the values of the VIFs, that multicollinearity is not an issue in the data, as this research applies

Table 5.7 TOL values (regression with capital structure variables as independent variables)

	DE	*EI*
OM	0.981	0.981
AT	0.982	0.982
ROE	0.981	0.981
REV	0.975	0.975
PRO	0.979	0.979
CAP	0.979	0.979
PB	0.982	0.982
PE	0.982	0.981

Source: Own presentation.

a very strict cut-off threshold, with a TOL > 0.8 = VIF of > 1.25 for the assessment of a regression model. It is, therefore, useful to potentially apply the variables in further analysis.

5.3 Regression Analysis

The results of the regression analysis are presented below. First, the stepwise forward regression results are shown, followed by the panel regression analysis results.

Stepwise Forward Regression

The results of the stepwise forward regression are shown below, first for the capital structure variables as dependent variables. The criterion for the inclusion of a variable in the regression table output is a p-value of at least 0.05. The regression statistics are depicted in Table 5.8 for the debt ratio (variable: DE).

The results show a total of seven variables as significant to be included in the model, with OM being the most important predictor. Generally, the ranking of the variables as indicated by the number of steps provided information on the importance of the variables (Kutner et al., 2005, pp. 364–365). This means that PE is the least important variable in the stepwise forward regression model for the debt ratio. With the exception of profitability growth (variable: PRO), all predicting performance variables were included. Similarly, Table 5.9 shows the results from stepwise forward regression for the interest coverage ratio (variable: EI).

Regarding the interest coverage ratio, only four variables showed sufficient significance for model inclusion: ROE, PB, OM, and AT. This means that four other variables (REV, PRO, CAP, and PE) are not able to significantly predict the interest coverage ratio. Similarly, stepwise

Table 5.8 Results for stepwise forward regression (debt ratio: DE)

Step	*Var*	R^2	*Adj.* R^2	*C(p)*	*AIC*	*RMSE*
1	OM	0.0051	0.0049	50.6742	-2424.3158	0.1802
2	REV	0.0085	0.0079	72.3311	-1915.2855	0.1810
3	AT	0.0145	0.0136	53.7566	-1933.5173	0.1805
4	PB	0.0177	0.0166	44.9624	-1940.9785	0.1802
5	ROE	0.0201	0.0187	35.6045	-1940.0126	0.1799
6	CAP	0.0210	0.0192	10.9908	-1915.8268	0.1792
7	PE	0.0226	0.0204	7.9310	-1918.8954	0.1791

Source: Own presentation.

Table 5.9 Results for stepwise forward regression (interest coverage ratio: EI)

Step	*Var*	R^2	*Adj.* R^2	*C(p)*	*AIC*	*RMSE*
1	ROE	0.0264	0.0262	104.1712	44911.6552	106.1084
2	PB	0.0385	0.0379	59.3361	44867.7736	105.4652
3	OM	0.0502	0.0494	11.8852	44772.1444	104.7808
4	AT	0.0529	0.0519	3.2587	44763.5138	104.6441

Source: Own presentation.

forward regression was also performed by using each of the performance variables as dependent variables, while the capital structure variables DE and EI were used for prediction. The results for all variables are depicted in Table 5.10.

The results for the stepwise forward regression are mixed. For OM and AT, both capital structure variables show a significant relation at the $p = 0.05$ level. In contrast, the remaining six variables only show a predictive relationship with either one of the capital structure variables, respectively.

Panel Regression Models

The regression analysis was performed with several types of panel regression models, specifically with fixed- and with random-effects regression. Other available regression models like regression with pooled cross-sectional data were not used, as pooled regression is deemed as less useful and more applicable for the evaluation of particular events (Wooldridge, 2013). The results for the fixed- and the random-effects regression are shown in Table 5.11 for DE as dependent variable. Given the results from the stepwise regression model, variable PRO was not used, as it was found as not significant.[1]

Table 5.10 Results for stepwise forward regression on the performance variables

Step	*Var*	R^2	*Adj.* R^2	$C(p)$	*AIC*	*RMSE*
OM						
1	EI	0.0217	0.0214	25.6386	2815.1869	0.3526
2	DE	0.0281	0.0276	3.0000	2792.6096	0.3515
AT						
1	EI	0.0068	0.0065	16.5705	7150.7712	0.6296
2	DE	0.0109	0.0103	3.0000	7135.3121	0.6283
ROE						
1	EI	0.0264	0.0262	0.2947	5276.3691	0.4942
REV						
1	DE	0.0014	0.0011	-33.2877	36927.9075	63.0272
PRO						
1	DE	0.0008	0.0005	-145.0854	34089.1797	25.8302
CAP						
1	DE	0.0013	0.0010	-270.0920	32405.7752	17.4456
PB						
1	EI	0.0134	0.0131	0.9335	17230.8668	2.4253
PE						
1	EI	0.0040	0.0037	1.4499	36409.6612	31.6470

Source: Own presentation.

Table 5.11 Fixed- and random-effects regression results for DE

Fixed-effects regression		*Random-effects regression*	
Dependent variable: DE			
OM	-0.012	OM	-0.005
	(0.008)		(0.008)
AT	0.014***	AT	0.003
	(0.005)		(0.005)
ROE	-0.006	ROE	-0.006
	(0.005)		(0.005)
REV	-0.00003	REV	-0.00005
	(0.00004)		(0.00004)
CAP	0.0001	CAP	0.0001
	(0.0002)		(0.0002)
PB	-0.0004	PB	0.0003
	(0.001)		(0.001)
PE	-0.00002	PE	-0.00002
	(0.0001)		(0.0001)
		Constant	0.175***
			(0.008)
Observations	3,207	Observations	3,207
R^2	0.004	R^2	0.004
Adjusted R^2	-0.127	Adjusted R^2	0.002
F statistic	1.636	F statistic	4.334
	(df = 7; 2834)		

Source: Own presentation.

Note: *p<0.1; **p<0.05; ***p<0.01

Similarly, a fixed-effects and random-effects regression were performed for EI as a dependent variable as well. In this case, even more variables were excluded from the panel regression model based on the results of the stepwise regression. Specifically, only the variables ROE, PB, OM, and AT were used as independent variables. The results are depicted in Table 5.12:

Based on the results, the Hausman test was then applied on the random- and the fixed-effects model. This provided evidence for the alternative hypothesis of one of the models being inconsistent. The Hausman test was calculated for both models, using DE and EI as dependent variable, respectively. The chi-squared using DE was 64.507, while the chi-squared value for the model that used EI was 22.752. Consequently, due to the test results, the fixed-effects model needs to be selected for analysis.

Evaluating the results from fixed-effects regression, it is evident that the majority of the variables are not significant to predict the debt ratio (variable: DE). Only AT was found to have significant predictability for the debt ratio. That result provides a contrast to the result from the stepwise forward regression model, since this analysis has indicated the inclusion of all but one variable (variable PRO was excluded). In the case of EI, there are a total of four variables that show a significant relationship: OM, AT, ROE, and PB. Consequently, the evidence is more pronounced for EI, instead of DE.

Table 5.12 Fixed- and random-effects regression results for EI

Fixed-effects regression		*Random-effects regression*	
Dependent variable: EI			
OM	37.167***	OM	36.331***
	(5.834)		(5.361)
AT	12.194***	AT	11.415***
	(3.570)		(3.191)
ROE	14.666***	ROE	18.226***
	(3.509)		(3.423)
PB	3.134***	PB	3.366***
	(0.862)		(0.769)
		Constant	5.459
			(4.286)
Observations	3,687	Observations	3,687
R^2	0.029	R^2	0.036
Adjusted R^2	-0.08	Adjusted R^2	0.034
F statistic	24.841***	F statistic	131.828***
	(df = 4; 3315)		

Source: Own presentation.

Note: *p<0.1; **p<0.05; ***p<0.01

In addition to the investigation of the role of performance variables to capital structure variables, the recursive relationship was also evaluated. For this purpose, and similar to the method for the stepwise regression, the capital structure variables DE and EI were regressed on each of the performance variables. Due to the low number of independent variables that are applicable for regression of the performance variables, no exclusion was performed based on the results of the stepwise regression. However, the results of the stepwise regression models will be discussed and compared with the panel regression model values.

The results for fixed-effects regression are shown in Table 5.13. Similarly, Table 5.14 depicts the random-effects regression results:

Similar to the regression models that are employed to evaluate the impact of performance variables on capital structure variables, the Hausman test was applied to the random- and fixed-effects regression model as well. The results of this test provide evidence for the alternative hypothesis of one of the models being inconsistent. The Hausman test was applied for the fixed- and random-effects regression models for each of the eight performance variables (test statistics for chi-squared are as follows: OM = 18.13, AT = 31.976, ROE = 14.671, REV = 2.0583, PRO = 2.0613, CAP = 1.0277, PB = 511.31, and PE = 18.823). Therefore, the test results imply that the fixed-effects model is more useful for the analysis.

The results provide a mixed picture. For the performance variables REV, PRO, CAP, and PE, no relationship to either of the two capital structure variables has been found. Therefore, the model implies that there is no impact of these variables at all. In contrast to that, OM, AT, and PB show a relationship with both capital structure variables. However, except for AT, the significance of the results is much stronger in the case of EI than for DE. Given the results of the stepwise regression models, the panel regression models give plausible results.

Generally, it can be stated that the predictive capability of performance variables is more pronounced for EI. In the case of ROE, a significant relationship was only found for EI but not for DE. This again confirms the strength of the results for EI.

5.4 Techniques for Group Comparison Analysis

The results shown above for the total dataset of listed firms from Germany have also been calculated for the subgroups that were defined with respect to differences in growth and profitability rates, industry differences, and size. This refers to the analysis of the capital structure on performance variables as well as the recursive relationship. In addition to the regressions on the particular subgroups, t-tests for mean differences across the subgroups are performed.

Table 5.13 Fixed-effects regression of capital structure variables on performance variables

	OM	*AT*	*ROE*	*REV*	*PRO*	*CAP*	*PB*	*PE*
DE	-0.062*	0.220***	-0.019	-8.005	2.143	1.323	0.453*	1.919
	(0.036)	(0.059)	(0.061)	(9.282)	(3.799)	(2.216)	(0.245)	(4.131)
EI	0.0004***	0.0004***	0.0005***	0.010	0.006	0.001	0.001***	-0.0003
	(0.0001)	(0.0001)	(0.0001)	(0.012)	(0.005)	(0.003)	(0.0003)	(0.006)
Observations	3,732	3,736	3,690	3,101	3,380	3,464	3,736	3,734
R^2	0.017	0.009	0.009	0.001	0.001	0.0001	0.006	0.0001
Adjusted R^2	-0.091	-0.099	-0.101	-0.133	-0.121	-0.119	-0.103	-0.109
F statistic	28.676***	16.071***	14.602***	0.741	0.864	0.230	9.499***	0.110
	(df = 2; 3362)	(df = 2; 3366)	(df = 2; 3320)	(df = 2; 2735)	(df = 2; 3012)	(df = 2; 3094)	(df = 2; 3366)	(df = 2; 3365)

Source: Own presentation.

Note: $^{*}p<0.1$; $^{**}p<0.05$; $^{***}p<0.01$

Table 5.14 Random-effects regression of capital structure variables on performance variables

	OM	*AT*	*ROE*	*REV*	*PRO*	*CAP*	*PB*	*PE*
DE	-0.013	0.103*	0.011	-13.500*	2.651	0.798	0.960***	-0.529
	(0.033)	(0.055)	(0.052)	(7.420)	(2.902)	(1.938)	(0.232)	(3.186)
EI	0.0004***	0.0004***	0.001***	0.005	0.003	0.0002	0.002***	0.012**
	(0.00005)	(0.0001)	(0.0001)	(0.011)	(0.005)	(0.003)	(0.0003)	(0.005)
Constant	0.005	0.625***	0.059***	16.656***	3.372***	4.781***	2.006***	17.898***
	(0.014)	(0.027)	(0.017)	(2.293)	(0.842)	(0.698)	(0.096)	(0.898)
Observations	3,732	3,736	3,690	3,101	3,380	3,464	3,736	3,734
R^2	0.017	0.007	0.014	0.004	0.001	0.001	0.010	0.0004
Adjusted R^2	0.016	0.006	0.013	0.003	0.0003	0.001	0.009	-0.0001
F statistic	64.316***	23.685***	54.584***	3.713	1.081	0.170	37.009***	5.777*

Source: Own presentation.

Note: $^{*}p<0.1$; $^{**}p<0.05$; $^{***}p<0.01$

Regressing Firm Performance Variables on Capital Structure Variables

The results for the fixed-effects regression are shown in Table 5.15 and Table 5.16, respectively, for the debt ratio (DE). Random-effects regression was also performed, but results presentation was skipped because the Hausman test for both types of models indicated that fixed-effects regression provides a superior way for the estimation. This is similar to the results for the entire dataset, where the Hausman test provided evidence in favour of the alternative hypothesis of one of the models being inconsistent. It is, therefore, not necessarily relevant to report the random-effects regression results.

The results of the fixed-effects regression analysis clearly show a number of differences in the ability of some performance variables in predicting the debt ratio depending on the subgroup. Whereas the dataset containing all groups only showed AT to be a significant predictor variable, selected datasets show a much larger set of significant predictor variables. Additionally, some relationships of predictor variables show different signs, depending on which subgroup is used. The results, which will be discussed later in this chapter, clearly imply that functional relationships of the variables in the model need to be distinguished with respect to subgroups in order to provide more depth to the analysis of the relationship between capital structure and firm performance.

Similar to the debt level (variable DE), the fixed-effects regression was also performed with respect to EI as dependent variable for all subsets. The results of these calculations are shown in Table 5.17 and Table 5.8:

The results of the fixed-effects regression using EI as a dependent variable are generally more homogeneous across subgroups. However, differences exist as well, which will be discussed later.

Regressing Capital Structure Variables on Firm Performance Variables

In addition to the relationship of performance variables on a particular capital structure variable as independent variable, the recursive relationship was assessed. This was performed for all groups that were distinguished on the basis of differences in revenue, profitability growth, and size differences. Also, the calculations were performed for all three main industries: industrials, technology, and consumer cyclical.

The results of these calculations are shown in Tables 5.19 to 5.26. It must be noted that the calculations were performed equally for all subsets been defined so far regarding the differences in revenue and profit growth, size, and industry classification.

Table 5.15 Fixed-effects regression of capital structure variable DE on performance variables (subsets for differences in revenue growth, profitability growth, and size differences)

	All firms	*High revenue growth*	*Low revenue growth*	*High profitability growth*	*Low profitability growth*	*Large (size)*	*Small (size)*
OM	-0.012	0.046***	0.041***	0.029**	0.037***	0.051***	0.019
	(0.008)	(0.013)	(0.012)	(0.012)	(0.013)	(0.015)	(0.012)
AT	0.014***	-0.027***	-0.010	-0.042***	0.008	-0.014*	-0.003
	(0.005)	(0.007)	(0.009)	(0.007)	(0.009)	(0.008)	(0.008)
ROE	-0.006	0.002	-0.016*	-0.024***	0.002	-0.043***	-0.0004
	(0.005)	(0.009)	(0.009)	(0.009)	(0.010)	(0.010)	(0.008)
REV	-0.00003	-0.0001	0.044***	0.0001	-0.0001**	-0.0002**	-0.00005
	(0.00004)	(0.0001)	(0.013)	(0.0001)	(0.0001)	(0.0001)	(0.0001)
CAP	0.0001	0.001*	0.001*	0.0002	0.0002	0.011	0.0003
	(0.0002)	(0.0003)	(0.0003)	(0.0002)	(0.0003)	(0.011)	(0.0002)
PB	-0.0004	-0.003*	-0.002	0.0004	-0.004**	-0.002	-0.001
	(0.001)	(0.002)	(0.002)	(0.002)	(0.002)	(0.002)	(0.002)
PE	-0.00002	0.0001	-0.0001	-0.0003**	-0.0001	-0.0002*	-0.0001
	(0.0001)	(0.0001)	(0.0001)	(0.0002)	(0.0001)	(0.0001)	(0.0001)
Observations	3,207	1,626	1,581	1,614	1,591	1,744	1,463
R^2	0.004	0.026	0.019	0.036	0.014	0.028	0.005
Adjusted R^2	-0.127	-0.081	-0.092	-0.080	-0.108	-0.087	-0.139
F statistic	1.636	5.661***	3.954***	7.721***	2.770***	6.444***	1.006
	(df = 7; 2834)	(df = 7; 1464)	(df = 7; 1419)	(df = 7; 1440)	(df = 7; 1416)	(df = 7; 1558)	(df = 7; 1277)

Source: Own presentation.

Note: $^{*}p<0.1$; $^{**}p<0.05$; $^{***}p<0.01$

Table 5.16 Fixed-effects regression of capital structure variable DE on performance variables (subsets for sector differences: industrials, technology, and consumer cyclical)

	All firms	*Industrials*	*Technology*	*Consumer cyclical*
OM	-0.012	0.049**	-0.022	0.037
	(0.008)	(0.020)	(0.027)	(0.036)
AT	0.014***	-0.008	0.015	-0.012
	(0.005)	(0.008)	(0.010)	(0.014)
ROE	-0.006	-0.00001	-0.016	-0.033
	(0.005)	(0.011)	(0.010)	(0.021)
REV	-0.00003	-0.00003	-0.0002	-0.0003
	(0.00004)	(0.00005)	(0.0001)	(0.0002)
CAP	0.0001	0.0002	0.0001	0.0002
	(0.0002)	(0.0002)	(0.001)	(0.001)
PB	-0.0004	-0.003	0.002	0.005
	(0.001)	(0.002)	(0.002)	(0.004)
PE	-0.00002	0.0001	0.0001	-0.0001
	(0.0001)	(0.0001)	(0.0002)	(0.0002)
Observations	3,207	706	698	423
R^2	0.004	0.018	0.014	0.020
Adjusted R^2	-0.127	-0.144	-0.131	-0.155
F statistic	1.636	1.621	1.194	1.069
	(df = 7; 2834)	(df = 7; 605)	(df = 7; 608)	(df = 7; 358)

Source: Own presentation.

Note: *p<0.1; **p<0.05; ***p<0.01

The results are, in principle, comparable to the results for the subsets calculations for the capital structure variables, as it was found that some subsets show very different results when compared to the results for the entire data of listed German firms. However, some of the subsets show comparable relationships, like the total firm data on the relevance of DE and EI for the particular performance variable.

The main finding from the calculation is that there is indeed, in some cases, a recursive relationship between firm performance and capital structure. Nevertheless, this relationship is not equally strong across all possible cases involving the defined variables, or even existing variables, as it depends on the way performance is being measured. For example, there is virtually no evidence for PE or CAP[1] and little evidence with respect to REV or ROE, especially regarding any predictability for DE.

However, there is a comparatively strong impact of capital structure variables on OM and AT. Interestingly, the sign of statistically significant relationships that were found is not equal across the subsets, with some showing a positive and some a negative relationship. This result is particularly interesting because it shows that statistically, a higher leverage level can either reduce or increase the operating margin or asset turnover. This

Table 5.17 Fixed-effects regression of capital structure variable EI on performance variables (subsets for differences in revenue growth, profitability growth, and size differences)

	All firms	*High revenue growth*	*Low revenue growth*	*High profitability growth*	*Low profitability growth*	*Large (size)*	*Small (size)*
OM	37.167***	19.862**	31.678***	35.791***	30.459***	34.902***	28.045***
	-5.834	-9.917	-6.482	-9.054	-6.871	-8.640	-7.575
AT	12.194***	6.398	7.612*	16.017***	0.116	14.750***	6.695
	-3.570	-5.148	-4.284	-4.913	-4.150	-4.360	-4.792
ROE	14.666***	18.707***	17.955***	27.879***	14.938***	2.943	22.390***
	-3.509	-6.553	-4.659	-6.100	-4.596	-5.610	-5.117
PB	3.134***	5.367***	2.742***	5.137***	2.737***	3.465***	2.736***
	(0.862)	-1.326	(0.910)	-1.204	(0.937)	-1.218	-1.026
Observations	3,687	1,578	1,51	1,712	1,644	1,868	1,69
R^2	0.029	0.027	0.045	0.058	0.029	0.023	0.033
Adjusted R^2	-0.080	-0.082	-0.066	-0.046	-0.084	-0.083	-0.084
F statistic	24.841***	9.759***	15.989***	23.775***	11.013***	9.834***	12.947***
	(df = 4; 3315)	(df = 4; 1419)	(df = 4; 1351)	(df = 4; 1540)	(df = 4; 1472)	(df = 4; 1684)	(df = 4; 1507)

Source: Own presentation.

Note: *p<0.1; **p<0.05; ***p<0.01

Table 5.18 Fixed-effects regression of capital structure variable EI on performance variables (subsets for sector differences: industrials, technology, and consumer cyclical)

	All firms	*Industrials*	*Technology*	*Consumer cyclical*
OM	37.167***	62.464***	91.134***	33.141
	-5.834	-10.317	-22.083	-28.813
AT	12.194***	6.875*	6.494	41.800***
	-3.570	-4.050	-8.295	-11.288
ROE	14.666***	10.485**	19.612**	12.819
	-3.509	-5.287	-8.748	-14.800
PB	3.134***	6.524***	4.614**	10.212***
	(0.862)	-1.253	-1.890	-3.104
Observations	3,687	869	720	485
R^2	0.029	0.096	0.066	0.062
Adjusted R^2	-0.080	-0.018	-0.061	-0.075
F statistic	24.841***	20.469***	11.154***	7.014***
	(df = 4; 3315)	(df = 4; 771)	(df = 4; 633)	(df = 4; 422)

Source: Own presentation.

Note: *p<0.1; **p<0.05; ***p<0.01

may imply managerial implications, as leverage may need to be applied differently depending on the subgroup.

Evaluating Mean Differences of Subsets

As it was found in the preceding paragraph that firms may exhibit different characteristics regarding the statistical relationships of capital structure and performance variables, it may be interesting to further investigate if these firms show significant mean differences regarding these variables. It may be argued that existing differences, for example, in the leverage of firms, may contribute to the findings. This would imply the existence of non-linear relationships, which are further investigated with the artificial neural network analysis in the next section of this thesis.

Given the large number of potential combinations for a t-test involving all capital structure and performance variables in combination with all the subgroups, some of the combinations were excluded from the analysis, and only the most relevant combinations for the analysis in this thesis were included in the t-test calculations. Specifically, only the variable DE was tested, as it is deemed the most central variable for capital structure research. Also, only OM and AT were selected as examples for performance variables to be used for the t-test. This was performed because of the results of the preceding section, where it was found that OM and AT showed comparatively good ability for predicting capital structure variables across the subgroups.

Table 5.19 Fixed-effects regression of capital structure variables on OM for all subsets

	All firms	*High revenue growth*	*Low revenue growth*	*High profitability growth*	*Low profitability growth*	*Large (size)*	*Small (size)*	*Industrials*	*Technology*	*Consumer cyclical*
DE	-0.062*	0.184***	0.128**	0.104**	0.113**	0.103**	-0.026	0.172***	-0.105	-0.021
	(0.036)	(0.054)	(0.054)	(0.053)	(0.048)	(0.042)	(0.058)	(0.065)	(0.068)	(0.066)
EI	0.0004***	0.0002***	0.001***	0.0004***	0.001***	0.0003***	0.0004***	0.001***	0.0004***	0.0001
	(0.0001)	(0.0001)	(0.0001)	(0.0001)	(0.0001)	(0.0001)	(0.0001)	(0.0001)	(0.0001)	(0.0001)
Observations	3,732	1,581	1,519	1,720	1,658	1,874	1,711	883	733	488
R^2	0.017	0.014	0.029	0.024	0.021	0.014	0.015	0.065	0.047	0.004
Adjusted R^2	-0.091	-0.094	-0.082	-0.083	-0.091	-0.092	-0.101	-0.048	-0.076	-0.136
F statistic	28.676***	10.094***	20.227***	18.829***	15.586***	11.913***	11.610***	27.142***	16.116***	0.918
	(df = 2; 3362)	(df = 2; 1424)	(df = 2; 1362)	(df = 2; 1550)	(df = 2; 1488)	(df = 2; 1692)	(df = 2; 1530)	(df = 2; 787)	(df = 2; 648)	(df = 2; 427)

Source: Own presentation.

Table 5.20 Fixed-effects regression of capital structure variables on AT for all subsets

	All firms	*High revenue growth*	*Low revenue growth*	*High profitability growth*	*Low profitability growth*	*Large (size)*	*Small (size)*	*Industrials*	*Technology*	*Consumer cyclical*
DE	0.220***	-0.418***	-0.096	-0.470***	-0.020	-0.236***	-0.007	0.143	0.370**	0.134
	(0.059)	(0.101)	(0.079)	(0.093)	(0.078)	(0.082)	(0.091)	(0.163)	(0.163)	(0.165)
EI	0.0004***	0.0002	0.0004**	0.0005***	0.00002	0.0004***	0.0003**	0.001**	0.0004*	0.001***
	(0.0001)	(0.0001)	(0.0002)	(0.0001)	(0.0002)	(0.0001)	(0.0001)	(0.0003)	(0.0002)	(0.0002)
Observations	3,736	1,581	1,520	1,721	1,659	1,874	1,715	883	734	488
R^2	0.009	0.015	0.005	0.028	0.0001	0.012	0.003	0.008	0.012	0.034
Adjusted R^2	-0.099	-0.093	-0.109	-0.078	-0.113	-0.093	-0.114	-0.112	-0.115	-0.101
F statistic	16.071***	10.581***	3.533**	22.611***	0.039	10.567***	2.347*	3.237**	4.079**	7.611***
	(df = 2; 3366)	(df = 2; 1424)	(df = 2; 1363)	(df = 2; 1551)	(df = 2; 1489)	(df = 2; 1692)	(df = 2; 1534)	(df = 2; 787)	(df = 2; 649)	(df = 2; 427)

Source: Own presentation.

Table 5.21 Fixed-effects regression of capital structure variables on ROE for all subsets

	All firms	*High revenue growth*	*Low revenue growth*	*High profitability growth*	*Low profitability growth*	*Large (size)*	*Small (size)*	*Industrials*	*Technology*	*Consumer cyclical*
DE	-0.019	0.094	-0.055	-0.035	0.106	-0.226***	0.054	0.207	-0.137	-0.271**
	(0.061)	(0.082)	(0.075)	(0.079)	(0.072)	(0.066)	(0.087)	(0.135)	(0.170)	(0.130)
EI	0.0005***	0.0004***	0.001***	0.001***	0.001***	0.0001	0.001***	0.001***	0.001***	0.0001
	(0.0001)	(0.0001)	(0.0002)	(0.0001)	(0.0001)	(0.0001)	(0.0001)	(0.0002)	(0.0002)	(0.0002)
Observations	3,690	1,578	1,511	1,713	1,645	1,868	1,693	869	720	485
R^2	0.009	0.012	0.020	0.028	0.012	0.009	0.019	0.021	0.027	0.015
Adjusted R^2	-0.101	-0.097	-0.093	-0.078	-0.101	-0.097	-0.098	-0.099	-0.101	-0.125
F statistic	14.602*** (df = 2; 3320)	8.331*** (df = 2; 1421)	13.842*** (df = 2; 1354)	22.473*** (df = 2; 1543)	9.229*** (df = 2; 1475)	7.791*** (df = 2; 1686)	14.387*** (df = 2; 1512)	8.314*** (df = 2; 773)	8.896*** (df = 2; 635)	3.174** (df = 2; 424)

Source: Own presentation.

Table 5.22 Fixed-effects regression of capital structure variables on REV for all subsets

	All firms	*High revenue growth*	*Low revenue growth*	*High profitability growth*	*Low profitability growth*	*Large (size)*	*Small (size)*	*Industrials*	*Technology*	*Consumer cyclical*
DE	-8.005	-22.677	0.109*	3.119	-21.502**	-26.325**	-6.384	-22.243	-17.191	-18.876
	-9.282	-14.094	(0.056)	-9.220	-10.759	-10.720	-11.200	-35.074	-14.850	-15.734
EI	0.010	-0.012	-0.00002	-0.007	0.044*	0.006	0.011	-0.013	0.005	0.002
	(0.012)	(0.019)	(0.0001)	(0.013)	(0.022)	(0.018)	(0.017)	(0.063)	(0.016)	(0.019)
Observations	3,101	1,581	1,520	1,558	1,540	1,684	1,393	704	653	408
R^2	0.001	0.002	0.003	0.0003	0.006	0.004	0.001	0.001	0.003	0.004
Adjusted R^2	-0.133	-0.107	-0.111	-0.121	-0.117	-0.115	-0.146	-0.155	-0.145	-0.164
F statistic	0.741 (df = 2; 2735)	1.382 (df = 2; 1424)	1.949 (df = 2; 1363)	0.242 (df = 2; 1389)	4.184** (df = 2; 1370)	3.292** (df = 2; 1503)	0.437 (df = 2; 1214)	0.213 (df = 2; 608)	0.751 (df = 2; 568)	0.777 (df = 2; 348)

Source: Own presentation.

Table 5.23 Fixed-effects regression of capital structure variables on PRO for all subsets

	All firms	*High revenue growth*	*Low revenue growth*	*High profitability growth*	*Low profitability growth*	*Large (size)*	*Small (size)*	*Industrials*	*Technology*	*Consumer cyclical*
DE	2.143	0.583	0.061	0.289	-0.095	-8.401*	5.959	-3.039	7.914*	1.258
	-3.799	-4.671	-3.605	-5.444	(0.620)	-4.855	-4.051	-8.042	-4.394	-12.548
EI	0.006	-0.002	0.015**	-0.0002	0.002	0.002	0.009	0.006	0.003	-0.009
	(0.005)	(0.006)	(0.008)	(0.008)	(0.001)	(0.008)	(0.006)	(0.016)	(0.005)	(0.015)
Observations	3,38	1,580	1,518	1,721	1,659	1,761	1,509	804	668	436
R^2	0.001	0.0001	0.003	0.00000	0.001	0.002	0.003	0.0005	0.006	0.001
Adjusted R^2	-0.121	-0.110	-0.111	-0.109	-0.112	-0.112	-0.131	-0.134	-0.137	-0.156
F statistic	0.864 (df = 2; 3012)	0.065 (df = 2; 1423)	1.931 (df = 2; 1361)	0.002 (df = 2; 1551)	0.859 (df = 2; 1489)	1.623 (df = 2; 1579)	2.024 (df = 2; 1329)	0.160 (df = 2; 708)	1.770 (df = 2; 583)	0.217 (df = 2; 376)

Source: Own presentation.

Table 5.24 Fixed-effects regression of capital structure variables on CAP for all subsets

	All firms	*High revenue growth*	*Low revenue growth*	*High profitability growth*	*Low profitability growth*	*Large (size)*	*Small (size)*	*Industrials*	*Technology*	*Consumer cyclical*
DE	1.323	3.510	2.445	0.122	0.626	-0.004	4.790	8.562	0.131	2.962
	-2.216	-2.406	-2.925	-3.164	-2.269	(0.059)	-3.874	-7.303	-3.269	-4.380
EI	0.001	-0.003	0.012**	-0.001	-0.0001	-0.00003	0.002	-0.002	0.004	0.002
	(0.003)	(0.003)	(0.006)	(0.004)	(0.005)	(0.0001)	(0.006)	(0.012)	(0.004)	(0.005)
Observations	3,464	1,557	1,468	1,653	1,556	1,874	1,590	798	704	461
R^2	0.0001	0.002	0.003	0.0001	0.0001	0.00004	0.001	0.002	0.002	0.001
Adjusted R^2	-0.119	-0.109	-0.115	-0.114	-0.122	-0.107	-0.126	-0.133	-0.133	-0.149
F statistic	0.230 (df = 2; 3094)	1.733 (df = 2; 1400)	2.195 (df = 2; 1311)	0.037 (df = 2; 1483)	0.039 (df = 2; 1386)	0.034 (df = 2; 1692)	0.783 (df = 2; 1410)	0.714 (df = 2; 702)	0.711 (df = 2; 619)	0.242 (df = 2; 400)

Source: Own presentation.

Table 5.25 Fixed-effects regression of capital structure variables on PB for all subsets

	All firms	*High revenue growth*	*Low revenue growth*	*High profitability growth*	*Low profitability growth*	*Large (size)*	*Small (size)*	*Industrials*	*Technology*	*Consumer cyclical*
DE	0.453*	-0.272	-0.054	0.302	-0.453	-0.185	0.710*	-0.502	1.828**	1.613***
	(0.245)	(0.392)	(0.374)	(0.383)	(0.348)	(0.296)	(0.425)	(0.519)	(0.723)	(0.593)
EI	0.001***	0.002***	0.002***	0.003***	0.002**	0.001***	0.002***	0.004***	0.003***	0.003***
	(0.0003)	(0.001)	(0.001)	(0.001)	(0.001)	(0.0005)	(0.001)	(0.001)	(0.001)	(0.001)
Observations	3,736	1,581	1,520	1,721	1,659	1,874	1,715	883	734	488
R^2	0.006	0.015	0.006	0.018	0.006	0.006	0.006	0.028	0.026	0.041
Adjusted R^2	-0.103	-0.093	-0.108	-0.089	-0.107	-0.100	-0.111	-0.089	-0.100	-0.094
F statistic	9.499***	10.521***	3.931**	13.937***	4.258**	5.274***	4.504**	11.438***	8.564***	9.119***
	(df = 2; 3366)	(df = 2; 1424)	(df = 2; 1363)	(df = 2; 1551)	(df = 2; 1489)	(df = 2; 1692)	(df = 2; 1534)	(df = 2; 787)	(df = 2; 649)	(df = 2; 427)

Source: Own presentation.

Table 5.26 Fixed-effects regression of capital structure variables on PE for all subsets

	All firms	*High revenue growth*	*Low revenue growth*	*High profitability growth*	*Low profitability growth*	*Large (size)*	*Small (size)*	*Industrials*	*Technology*	*Consumer cyclical*
DE	1.919	1.558	-5.674	-3.761	-4.029	-7.553	-1.329	8.964	4.652	-5.935
	-4.131	-5.437	-5.223	-4.257	-5.768	-4.959	-5.067	-9.894	-9.748	-9.782
EI	-0.0003	0.007	0.015	0.024***	-0.002	0.010	0.012	-0.006	0.006	-0.007
	(0.006)	(0.007)	(0.011)	(0.006)	(0.012)	(0.008)	(0.008)	(0.019)	(0.011)	(0.012)
Observations	3,734	1,581	1,520	1,720	1,659	1,874	1,713	883	734	488
R^2	0.0001	0.001	0.002	0.012	0.0003	0.003	0.002	0.001	0.001	0.001
Adjusted R^2	-0.109	-0.109	-0.112	-0.096	-0.113	-0.104	-0.116	-0.119	-0.129	-0.139
F statistic	0.110 (df = 2; 3365)	0.480 (df = 2; 1424)	1.589 (df = 2; 1363)	9.479*** (df = 2; 1550)	0.248 (df = 2; 1489)	2.222 (df = 2; 1692)	1.312 (df = 2; 1532)	0.489 (df = 2; 787)	0.232 (df = 2; 649)	0.301 (df = 2; 427)

Source: Own presentation.

As it was found in the preceding paragraph that firms may exhibit different characteristics regarding the statistical relationships of capital structure and performance variables, it may be interesting to further investigate if these firms show significant mean differences regarding these variables. It may be argued that existing differences, for example, in the leverage of firms, may contribute to the findings. This would imply the existence of non-linear relationships, which are further investigated with the artificial neural network analysis in the next section.

Given the large number of potential combinations for a t-test involving all capital structure and performance variables in combination with all the subgroups, some of the combinations were excluded from the analysis, and only the most relevant combinations for the analysis in this thesis were included in the t-test calculations. Specifically, only the variable DE was tested, as it is deemed the most central variable for capital structure research. Also, only OM and AT were selected as examples for performance variables to be used for the t-test. This was performed because of the results of the preceding section, where it was found that OM and AT showed comparatively good ability for predicting capital structure variables across the subgroups.

The t-test values depicted in Table 5.27 provided the conclusion that for all subgroups and for all variables, a statistically significant difference in the mean level exists. The differences exist in the comparison of each sample to the whole population, that is, the total firm sample. This implies that differences in the average level of the variables exist across the subgroups. However, it needs to be mentioned that there is some deviation in the level by which the magnitude of the difference in the sample mean level differs from the statistical level of the 95 percent confidence intervals. For example, the small firm sample's mean leverage level (DE) is close to the level of the entire population.

Given the results, it is possible that non-linearities in the relationships between the variables exist, so a linear regression methodology may not provide the best approach to the analysis of the data. The artificial neural network analysis is deemed to be better able to capture potentially existing non-linearities in the analysis of the data (Pao, 2008), which is investigated in the next section.

Artificial Neural Network Analysis

An artificial neural network analysis (ANN) was calculated as an additional tool for assessing the relationship between capital structure and firm performance, as well as a potential recursive relationship. Given the results achieved so far, the ANN is considered particularly useful in the investigation of non-linear relationships in the data.

Table 5.27 Results for mean group differences (t-test) for variables DE, OM, and AT across all subgroups (subsets for differences in revenue growth, profitability growth, size differences, and top three German industries)

Group	*t-value*	*Df*	*p-value*	*Mean total sample*	*Mean subgroup*
Variable: DE					
High revenue growth	3.8857	1658	0.000106	0.1596665	0.1766743
Low revenue Growth	3.1234	1659	0.001819	0.1596665	0.1738379
High profitability growth	2.9233	1822	0.003506	0.1596665	0.1719661
Low profitability growth	1.0702	1825	0.2847	0.1596665	0.1641897
Large (size)	3.8936	1966	0.0001021	0.1596665	0.1752533
Small (size)	-2.1386	1962	0.03259	0.1596665	0.1508708
Industrials	-4.9123	935	0.000001062	0.1596665	0.1371974
Technology	-6.4148	809	0.00000000002	0.1596665	0.1242523
Consumer cyclical	3.066	534	0.002279	0.1596665	0.186595
Variable: OM					
High revenue growth	2.0168	1654	0.04387	0.01861414	0.03655303
Low revenue growth	-2.5119	1651	0.0121	0.01861414	-0.006577318
High profitability growth	1.1874	1818	0.2352	0.01861414	0.02940831
Low profitability growth	-1.7027	1815	0.08879	0.01861414	0.003712149
Large (size)	4.683	1965	0.000003021	0.01861414	0.05203684
Small (size)	-4.3919	1952	0.00001184	0.01861414	-0.02487079
Industrials	0.90548	936	0.3654	0.01861414	0.02645799
Technology	0.40033	808	0.689	0.01861414	0.02192758
Consumer cyclical	1.9235	534	0.05494	0.01861414	0.03557684
Variable: AT					
High revenue growth	8.6504	1658	0,000000000000002	0.6243914	0.7669468
Low revenue growth	-7.2616	1659	0.0000000000005	0.6243914	0.5253395
High profitability growth	7.8	1824	0.00000000000001	0.6243914	0.7440569
Low profitability growth	-8.3603	1825	0.0000000000000002	0.6243914	0.5152706
Large (size)	2.4014	1966	0.01642	0.6243914	0.6571371
Small (size)	0.39145	1964	0.6955	0.6243914	0.6302529
Industrials	5.4084	935	0.00000008079	0.6243914	0.7297754
Technology	3.8987	809	0.0001047	0.6243914	0.7077388
Consumer cyclical	5.6627	535	0.00000002435	0.6243914	0.8013302

Source: Own presentation.

Due to the complexity of employing sophisticated models like the ANN and the number of potential parameter combinations in the dataset, a selection was made regarding the capital structure variable by limiting the analysis to the investigation of the determinants to leverage (DE) on the basis of the performance variables. Similarly, the recursive relationship was only investigated for the operating margin (OM). This decision was made on the basis of the results of the panel regression, where the group distinction showed OM to be a relatively important variable across the subsets.

Based on the use of two hidden layers with five and three neurons, respectively, the ANN model was calculated by using the performance variables as input variables and the debt ratio as output. This model is shown in Figure 5, with the lines in black depicting the connection of the layers with their weights, while the blue lines provide information on the basis that is added to each of the steps:

While Figure 5.1 cannot be interpreted in detail with respect to the weights or regarding the relationship between the variables and their

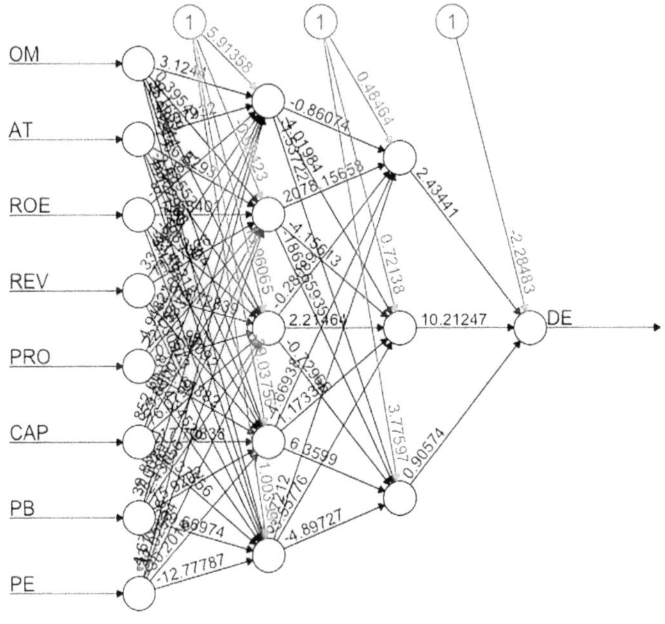

Figure 5.1 ANN model using performance variables as regression parameters for the debt ratio (DE)

ability for predictability, it is useful to demonstrate the logic of the analysis of the ANN approach. As the model is based on using test data as a share of the total data in order to perform predictions, it is relevant to investigate how the ANN model is able to make predictions. The accuracy of the predictions was assessed as well. This was performed by comparing real values with predicted values, as stated in Figure 5.2, where the circles in the graphic show the model predictions. The line in the graph can be used to assess the quality of the predictions made by the model. As can be seen, there is a relatively low level of alignment or a relatively small fit of the predicted data to the regression line.[2]

The result gives evidence to the argument that the model's performance variables are lacking in their ability to explain the debt ratio. This may not imply the irrelevance of particular variables in explaining the debt ratio, but it shows that the model itself does not account for other influences adequately. In this sense, it must also be mentioned that the results for R^2 in the regression equations also showed very small values. That equally implies that much of the variance of the dependent variable

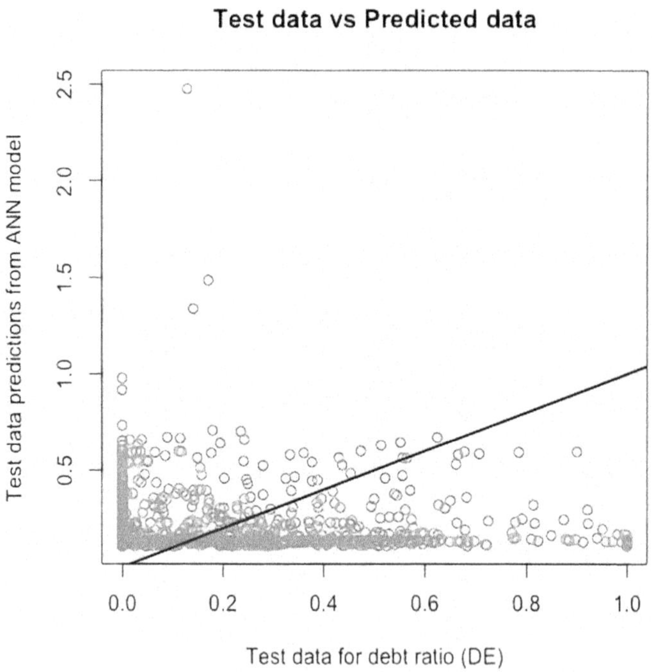

Figure 5.2 ANN model predictions versus test data for the debt ratio (DE)

(DE) is not explained by the independent (performance) variables. A fundamental concern in the quantitative analysis performed so far in this thesis was the issue of non-linear relationships in the data. Therefore, the ANN model was evaluated with respect to the generalised weights (GW) of the performance variables. These are shown in Figures 7 and 8 regarding their responsiveness towards DE.

The results for responsiveness imply that particular ranges for the values of variables can lead to relatively large deviations in the dependent variable. Given that there are significant mean differences in the mean of the variables across different subgroups, it can be argued that different levels of performance, typical for some groups of firms in the data, in combination with non-linearities in the data relationships, are making it difficult to adequately predict results.

Similar to the results for DE, the ANN model was also calculated by using the operating margin OM as a dependent variable in the regression

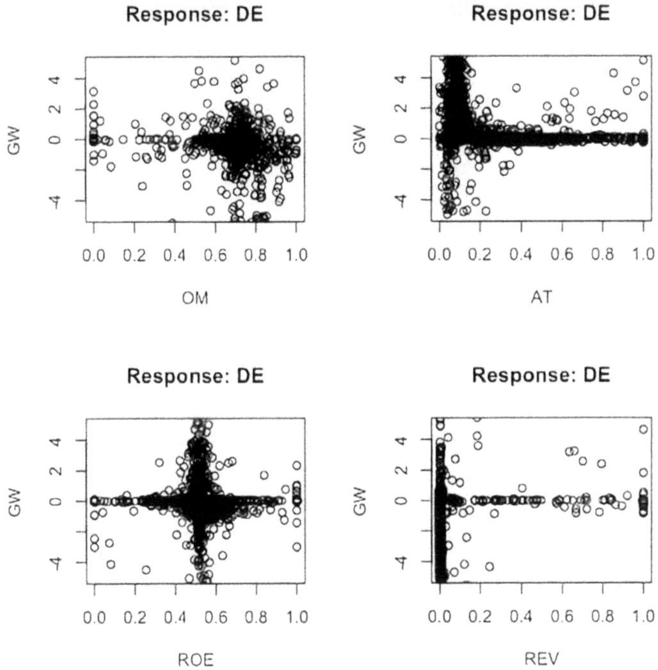

Figure 5.3 Generalised weights response of OM, AT, ROE, and REV on DE in the ANN model framework

Source: Own presentation.

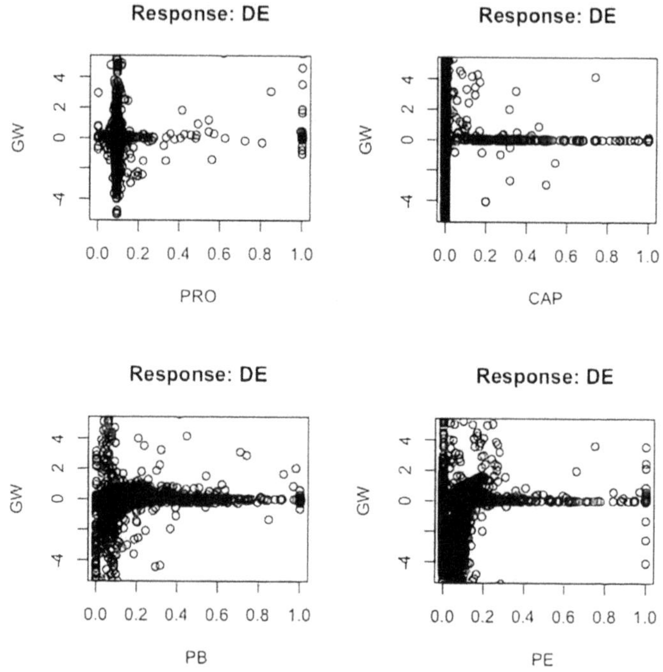

Figure 5.4 Generalised weights response of PRO, CAP, PB, and PE on DE in the ANN model framework

Source: Own presentation.

equation. The results, depicted in Figure 5.5, show equally that the model predictions are rather lacking in the ability to adequately predict the dependent variable. Therefore, much of the variability of OM remains unexplained when only DE and EI are used as explanatory values.

Additionally, the issue of non-linearities in the data was also used on the basis of the responsiveness of the generalised weights in the ANN model regarding the independent variables DE and EI. This is shown in Figure 5.6. Compared to the variability of the performance variables, as shown above, there is also a visible level of responsiveness in the data. Therefore, the current level of the independent variables DE and EI is not irrelevant to the response of OM in the model. However, it is interesting to point out that the response of DE to OM is smaller in comparison.

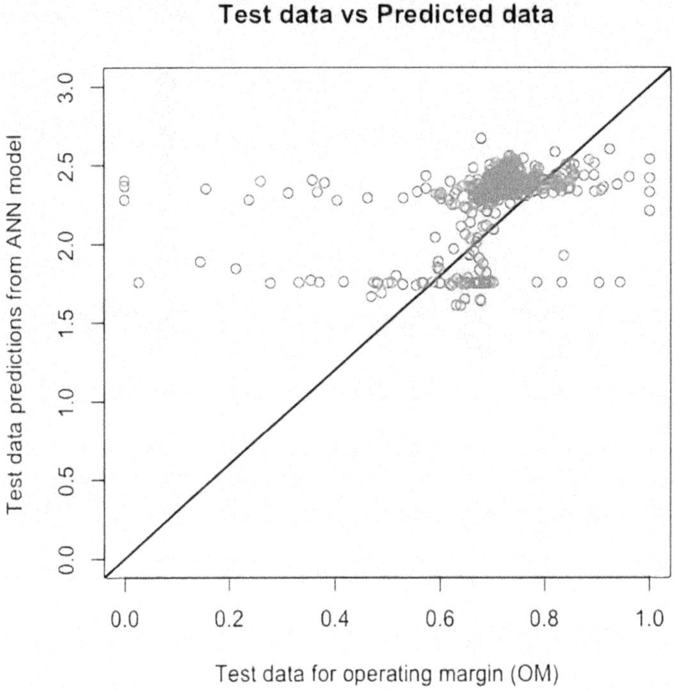

Figure 5.5 ANN model predictions versus test data for the operating margin

Source: Own presentation.

5.6 Evaluating Results and Facilitating Discussion

Based on the results shown so far in this chapter, an evaluation and discussion will be provided in order to align the findings with the state of the literature. Also, answers to the central research questions will be provided. This will be performed by discussing, firstly, the impact of firm performance on capital structure. Secondly, the recursive relationship will be addressed. A particular emphasis is placed in terms of the results of the group comparison because of the ability of this distinction to show how relevant a distinguished analysis is to the topic.

The Impact of Business Performance on Capital Structure

The first research question refers to the investigation of the potential impact of business performance on the capital structure choice of firms.

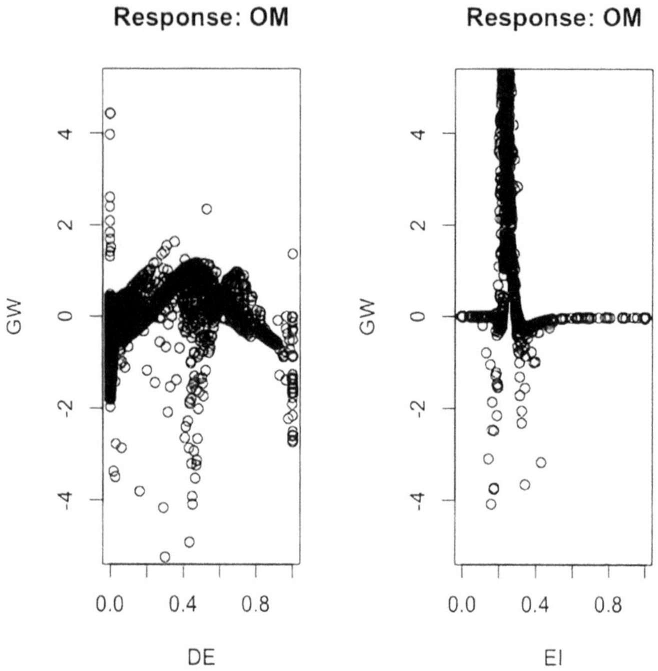

Figure 5.6 Generalised weights response of DE and EI on OM in the ANN model framework

Source: Own presentation.

Such research is conducted by a variety of authors (e.g., Frank & Goyal, 2003; Goddard et al., 2005; Zeitun & Tian, 2014). Methodically, it must be mentioned here that existing research uses various ways of measuring performance. Therefore, predictions regarding the influence of business performance on capital structure choice are performed quite differently. For the purpose of this thesis, a set of variables for measuring performance was defined and tested regarding its predictive ability. Hereby, selected performance variables that may show too much correlation were excluded from calculations to enhance predictive capabilities.

The results of the entire set of data from German-listed firms in the period from 2008 to 2019 showed little indication for the predictive capabilities of selected performance variables for the debt ratio but also for the interest coverage ratio. Only asset turnover was found to have a statistically significant positive relationship with the debt ratio. The result implies that for the total firm data, the evidence for an influence of performance on capital structure choice is rather poor. It is, therefore, not possible to draw meaningful conclusions on the validity of mayor capital structure theories, as these could neither be rejected nor directly confirmed by the results. In contrast to the results of the entire set of firms, group analysis provided more insight into the relationship between business performance and capital structure choice. For example, the debt ratio of large firms was found to be more responsive to performance variables. Interestingly, large firms' performance variables show both positive and negative relationships. For example, the operating margin is positively related to the debt ratio, whereas ROE, PE, and revenue growth show a negative relationship. This may imply that large firms use debt to further grow profitable business opportunities, as exemplified by an increasing operating margin. On the other hand, debt may also be helpful and, therefore, used by large firms in order to finance further investments that are necessary when the firm faces problems growing its revenue in the case of lower equity returns. The results confirm the notion of Frank and Goyal (2003) that large firms have more reputation in the debt markets and are, therefore, better equipped to use debt in the capital structure. This higher use of debt in the capital structure of large firms was found empirically as well as with the t-test, by which mean differences have been evaluated. The results, therefore, provide evidence for the applicability of the existence of market restrictions on the supply of capital, as pointed out, for example, by Campello et al. (2010). It can also be argued that asymmetric costs may be of relevance as well, particularly as it was found that the performance of small firms has no impact on their debt ratio. It is possible that superior performance cannot be used effectively to signal the quality of the firm and to obtain more debt capital for smaller firms (Ross, 1977).

Grouping companies based on their revenue or profit growth reveals a certain level of correlation between performance indicators and capital structure decisions. Although this connection is not observed in the majority of cases, there are some exceptions, especially among firms with exceptionally high profitability growth. These firms demonstrate that performance may not necessarily be positively associated with leverage. In fact, for companies in this group, a decrease in return on equity (ROE) and asset turnover led to a significant increase in their debt ratio.

Interestingly, high-growth and highly profitable firms are in a superior position, which allows them to utilise additional debt to fund their activities. This approach can help to sustain their high profitability levels, indicating that their capital structure decision is influenced by their growth potential and the potential benefits of additional debt financing. These findings are consistent with those of Eriotis et al. (2002), who also observed a negative correlation between profitability and debt ratio. While the relationship between performance and capital structure is complex, as evidenced by the empirical results shown so far, this research highlights the importance of considering a company's unique position (including sector and size issues) and potential when making capital structure decisions. While a high level of leverage may not always be beneficial, firms with strong growth potential may benefit from taking on additional debt to fund activities that will help them maintain their position in the market.

With respect to industry distinctions, the results are similar to the results of the total dataset in the sense that performance variables show an impact on capital structure choice. An observable impact was found for industrial and technology firms regarding a positive relationship between the operating margin and the ROE and the interest coverage ratio. This may show the existence of some firms from these groups with a comparatively good profitability and cash flow situation and a relatively low need to raise additional debt. Indeed, industrial and technology firms show a rather low debt level compared to consumer cyclical firms that potentially require more debt to finance their business activities.

The Impact of Capital Structure on Business Performance

The impact of capital structure on business performance was also assessed. This was performed by using each of the performance variables as a dependent variable, while the capital structure variables were used as independent variables. Here, the impact of leverage on the operating margin is very pronounced in the dataset for all firms. This is similarly found for asset turnover as a dependent variable as well, albeit in a positive direction. However, with the exception of PB, no significant impact of leverage on other performance variables was detected.

The results are, therefore, rather mixed with respect to the entire dataset. It can be stated that the direction of the functional relationship depends on the type of metric that is used for assessing performance. Interestingly, for particular groups of firms with a higher level of debt in the capital structure, such as large firms or firms in the consumer cyclical segment, performance is reduced with higher leverage. This can be observed regarding the performance measured with metrics including return on equity (ROE) and revenue growth (REV), although the results are not all statistically significant. Also, regarding AT as a dependent variable, some groups show a negative impact, while others show a positive impact of a change in leverage. This again shows that firms' performance reacts differently. It is, therefore, not possible to draw general conclusions from the results.

There are also other groups, in addition to large firms and firms in the consumer cyclical sector, where particular performance variables are negatively impacted by a higher level of leverage. Nevertheless, in general, most results do not show a significant relationship in fixed-effects regression equation results. The most convincing argument can be made with respect to large firms, as for most performance variables, a negative relationship was found in the case of a change in leverage. It is argued that these firms are best positioned to use leverage, as stated by Frank and Goyal (2003), which is confirmed by the t-tests for the sample. However, the data imply that the increase in leverage may lower overall performance.

In essence, there are cases in the data in which a relationship between capital structure and performance variables, including a recursive relationship, was found. However, there are no convincing findings that point towards the broad existence of such relationships. With the exception of firms that are distinguished by size, the findings call for further research to be carried out. In this regard, it must be mentioned that the ANN model has implied the existence of non-linear relationships among variables within the data. Therefore, the methodology applied must be refined in further investigations.

Discussion of Limitations of the Analysis

There are a number of limitations to the analysis, which will be pointed out in this final section of the chapter. These include issues concerning timing and adjustments, data issues, and model concerns.

Timing and Adjustments

The analysis presented in this book may be limited due to the time required for firms to adjust their capital structure. Strebulaev (2007) notes that infrequent large adjustments in the capital structure towards the target level are common, particularly for publicly traded large enterprises. This may be due to frictions that make firms hesitant to adjust their target leverage ratios. The slow adjustment of a particular structure in the balance sheet, like in the case of the capital structure, is more common for larger firms and is also found regarding other balance sheet positions, such as the level of cash that firms hold (Gao et al., 2013; Jiang & Lie, 2016).

It is important to note that the presence of these frictions may lead to a slower adjustment of the capital structure towards the target level, which in turn may affect the results of the analysis. Therefore, the results obtained from this study should be interpreted with caution, given these limitations. One possible way to address this limitation is by taking a deeper view over time, such as by using forward lags in the quantitative analysis, like in the regressions. Future work on the topic may benefit from focusing particularly on these issues to provide a more comprehensive understanding of the relationship between the capital structure and firm performance.

Data Issues and missing Data

The issue of missing data is a significant concern in this study, and it has been established that incomplete metrics in the panel dataset can lead to a decrease in the results' ability to explain real-world phenomena, ultimately reducing their reliability. The presence of missing data in empirical research that utilises financial metrics or balance sheet data is not uncommon, and it poses significant challenges in data analysis. The potential impact of missing data can be severe, as the data that are missing may be systematically related to the outcome variable, leading to bias in the analysis. Moreover, missing data can result in a decrease in the sample size, which reduces the statistical power of the analysis and the ability to detect meaningful relationships between variables.

Therefore, dealing with missing data in research is crucial, including the issue of dealing with extreme data points, which have been winsorised for practical purposes, as suggested in the empirical literature within other studies (Braun et al., 2017; Habib et al., 2013). Nevertheless, the availability of other methods must be mentioned (Ang, 2021), including different assumptions for the cut-off point used in the winsorisation of the data as well. It is possible that different methods may lead to different outcomes as well; however, it can be assumed that this risk is rather low. Nevertheless, higher-quality data are encouraged for future research on the topic.

For instance, the study of Vătavu (2015) is an example of this problem, where missing data resulted in issues regarding the statistical significance of the regression equations. Furthermore, the use of the winsorisation approach to address outliers in the data introduces a subjective element to the computational approach. It is worth mentioning that truncation is another method for addressing outliers in the data. However, it also suffers from being a subjective method. The approach to dealing with outliers in the data may impact the results of the analysis, and this should be taken into account when interpreting the results.

To address the issue of missing data, various imputation techniques can be used. One common approach is to use mean imputation, where the missing values are replaced with the mean value of the variable. However, this method can lead to biased estimates, especially if the data are not missing at random. Other approaches, such as multiple imputations or regression imputations, can provide better results. Future research may also focus on developing new techniques to address the issue of missing data and enhance the reliability of empirical studies.

Model Concerns

As mentioned by Pao (2008), research on capital structure may be impacted by the presence of non-linear relationships in the data. This critique is confirmed by the results of the ANN modelling approach in this thesis as well. It was shown that the response of the variable that is used as a dependent variable in the regression equation can be different in magnitude, depending on the range of the dependent variables used in the calculation. Also, the overall ability of the model to explain relationships is rather low. Further research is encouraged to shed more light on these issues, especially regarding the relationship in which capital structure variables are used to predict firm performance.

Other technical problems with the analysis can also be pointed out. For example, a common problem in capital structure research is the incorporation of non-financial liabilities as a type of debt (Welch, 2011). Whereas values from the financial statements are used for the construction and operationalisation of variables, the existence of non-financial debt may, in some cases, lead to lower values for the leverage of the firm. That, in turn, may lead to problems in the analysis of the relationship between firm performance and capital structure as well.

Notes

1 Nevertheless, a calculation with the inclusion of this variable was also performed, providing similar results. This is potentially the result of very low collinearity between the predictors, as was also shown by the low VIF and TOL values for the predictors as well.

2 It can be mentioned that a full alignment is equal to a mean-squared error value of zero.

Conclusion

In this monograph, the inverse relationship between capital structure and firm performance was investigated, focusing on publicly listed German companies over a period from 2008 to 2019. This study employed a substantial dataset of 361 firms, excluding those in the financial services sector due to the configuration of their capital structures. The study employed a variety of analytical methods, including regression models and artificial neural network (ANN) analysis, to achieve its objectives.

The findings obtained from the research show that while certain performance variables like operating margin, asset turnover, return on equity, and price-to-book ratio significantly predict the interest coverage ratio, they predict the debt ratio less consistently. The analysis highlighted the differences in capital structure dynamics across firm sizes and industries, showing a more pronounced response to performance variables from larger firms. This supports the suggestion that larger firms have superior financing options in comparison to smaller firms. The study also found evidence of a recursive relationship between capital structure and performance, suggesting that not only does capital structure influence performance, but efficiency can also impact capital structure decisions. However, this relationship is quite complex and varies significantly across different firm groups.

This research fills the gap in the empirical literature on capital structure by exploring the bidirectional relationship between capital structure and business performance. It underscores the necessity for more nuanced and differentiated samples in future research to better understand these dynamics. The findings also indicate the potential for non-linear relationships, suggesting in comparison to traditional linear models that may not fully capture the complexities of these interactions.

Additionally, the study highlighted the importance of considering institutional factors including economic, legal, and cultural differences, when analysing capital structures across different countries. This calls for further research that will cover a broader range of companies and

DOI: 10.4324/9781003545194-7

sectors to gain a comprehensive understanding of how these dynamics vary globally.

For practitioners, this study offers a valuable insight into how optimising capital structures can enhance firm's performance. We encourage managers to take into account industry-specific factors and the unique dynamics of their companies when making financing decisions. The study's findings suggest that leveraging their particular subgroup's characteristics can lead to better capital structure optimisation and to its improved performance.

The use of ANN models in this study also suggests the presence of non-linear relationships in the data, which managers should be aware of when applying these insights to their specific contexts. This further complicates the topic of optimising capital structure and highlights the need for additional theoretical research and practical experience to fully understand these dynamics.

Managers should take into account these unique factors that influence their industry and firm size, when they make capital structure decision. It is critical to consider other factors beyond those examined in the study, which include: market conditions and the competitive environment, to optimise capital structure and maximise potential growth. Additionally, awareness of potential non-linear relationships in the data can help managers make more precise decisions.

Overall, this monograph bridges the gap between theory and practice in the study of capital structure and firm performance. By providing a comprehensive analysis that is both academically rigorous and practically applicable, it enhances our understanding of these critical business dynamics and contributes to more effective and strategic financial decision-making. The study's significance extends beyond academic and managerial circles, offering valuable implications for investors, regulators, and other stakeholders in ensuring transparent and efficient financial markets.

References

Abdou, H. A., Kuzmic, A., Pointon, J., & Lister, R. J. (2012). Determinants of Capital Structure in the Uk Retail Industry: A Comparison of Multiple Regression and Generalized Regression Neural Network. *Intelligent Systems in Accounting, Finance and Management, 19*(3), 151–169. https://doi.org/10.1002/isaf.1330.

Abdou, H. A., Pointon, J., & El-Masry, A. (2012). Predicting creditworthiness in retail banking with limited scoring data. *Knowledge-Based Systems, 26*, 70–81. https://doi.org/10.1016/j.knosys.2011.06.012.

Acharya, V. V., Cooley, T., Richardson, M., & Walter, I. (2011). *Dodd-Frank act and Basel III: Intentions, unintended consequences, and lessons for emerging markets.* ADBI Working Paper Series.

Achtenhagen, L., Naldi, L., & Melin, L. (2010). "Business Growth" – Do practitioners and scholars really talk about the same thing? *Entrepreneurship Theory and Practice, 34*(2), 289–316.

Acs, Z. J., Parsons, W., & Tracy, S. (2008). *High-impact firms: Gazelles revisited.* Office of Advocacy, U.S. Small Business Administration.

Akerlof, G. A. (1970). The market for "Lemons": Quality uncertainty and the market mechanism. *The Quarterly Journal of Economics, 84*(3), 488–500.

Albrecht, W. S., Albrecht, C. O., & Albrecht, C. C. (2008). *Fraud examination.* Thomson/South-Western.

Albrecht, W. S., Albrecht, C. O., Albrecht, C. C., & Zimbelman, M. F. (2011). *Fraud examination* (4th ed.). South-Western Cengage Learning.

Alchian, A. A. (1950a). Uncertainty, evolution, and economic theory. *Journal of Political Economy, 58*(3), 211–221.

Aldrich, H. E. (1999). *Organizations evolving.* Sage Publications.

Alibaba annual report. (2022). Alibaba Group. https://static.alibabagroup.com/reports/fy2022/ar/ebook/en/22/index.html

Almus, M. (2000). What characterizes a fast-growing firm? *Applied Economics, 32*(10), 1347–1358.

Al-Najjar, B. (2013). The financial determinants of corporate cash holdings: Evidence from some emerging markets. *International Business Review, 22*(1), 77–88. https://doi.org/10.1016/j.ibusrev.2012.02.004

Altman, E. I. (1984). A further empirical investigation of the bankruptcy cost question. *The Journal of Finance, 39*(4), 1067–1089.

Amat, O., & Perramon, J. (2010). Innovation and quality management: The experience of Spanish firms. *Total Quality Management & Business Excellence*, *21*(1), 51–58.

Ang, A. (2021). *Asset management: A systematic approach to factor investing*. Oxford University Press.

Ansoff, H. I. (1965). *Corporate strategy: An analytic approach to business policy for growth and expansion*. McGraw-Hill.

Ansoff, H. I. (1988). *The New Corporate Strategy*. New York: Wiley.

Anyadike-Danes, M., Bonner, K., Hart, M., & Mason, C. (2009). *Measuring business growth: High-growth firms and their contribution to employment in the UK*. National Endowment for Science, Technology and the Arts (NESTA).

Apple. (2022). *Apple's green bond allocation report*. Apple Inc.

Arner, D. W., Barberis, J., & Buckley, R. P. (2015). "The Evolution of Fintech: A New Post-Crisis Paradigm?" *Georgetown Journal of International Law*, *47*, 1271.

Arnold, G. (2008). *Corporate financial management*. Pearson Education.

Asian Development Bank. (2022). *Asian bond monitor*. Retrieved from ADB.

Ayyagari, M., Demirguc-Kunt, A., & Maksimovic, V. (2010). Formal versus informal finance: Evidence from China. *The Review of Financial Studies*, *23*(8), 3048–3097.

Backhaus, K., Erichson, B., Plinke, W., & Weiber, R. (2018). *Multivariate Analysemethoden: Eine anwendungsorientierte Einführung*. Springer.

Baker, M., & Wurgler, J. (2002). Market timing and capital structure. *The Journal of Finance*, *57*(1), 1–32. https://doi.org/10.1111/1540-6261.00414.

Baltes-Götz, B. (2018). *Lineare Regressionsanalyse mit SPSS*. University of Trier.

Barney, J. B. (1991). Firm resources and sustained competitive advantage. *Journal of Management*, *17*(1), 99–120.

Barringer, B. R., & Jones, F. F. (2004). Achieving rapid growth – revisiting the managerial capacity problem. *Journal of Developmental Entrepreneurship*, *9*(1), 73–87.

Barringer, B. R., Jones, F. F., & Neubaum, D. O. (2005). A quantitative content analysis of the characteristics of rapid-growth firms and their founders. *Journal of Business Venturing*, *20*(5), 663–664.

Baum, C. F., Schafer, D., & Talavera, O. (2006). *The effects of short-term liabilities on profitability: The case of Germany*. DIW Discussion Paper 635, 1–23.

Beers, C., & Zand, F. (2014). R&D cooperation partner diversity and innovation performance: An empirical analysis. *Journal of Product Innovation Management*, *31*, 292–312.

Belitz, H., Lejpras, A., & Priem, M. (2019). Research and development abroad: German companies focus on strengths similar to those at home. *DIW Weekly Report*, *9*(35/36), 313–321. https://doi.org/10.18723/diw_dwr:2019-35-2.

Belleflamme, P., Lambert, T., & Schwienbacher, A. (2014). Crowdfunding: Tapping the right crowd. *Journal of Business Venturing*, *29*(5), 585–609.

Belsley, D. A., Kuh, E., & Welsch, R. E. (1980). *Regression diagnostics: Identifying influential data and sources of collinearity*. John Wiley & Sons.

Bergauer, A. (2001). *Erfolgreiches Krisenmanagement in der Unternehmung. Eine empirische Analyse*. Berlin: ESV.

Berger, A. N. (1995). The relationship between capital and earnings in banking. *Journal of Money Credit and Banking*, *27*(2), 432–456. https://doi.org/10.2307/2077877.

Berger, A. N., & Bonaccorsi di Patti, E. (2006). Capital structure and firm performance: A new approach to testing agency theory and an application to the banking industry. *Journal of Banking & Finance*, *30*(4), 1065–1102. https://doi.org/10.1016/j.jbankfin.2005.05.015.

Bertrand, M., & Schoar, A. (2003). Managing with style: The effect of managers on firm policies. *The Quarterly Journal of Economics*, *118*(4), 1169–1208.

Bessant, J., Phelps, B., & Adams, R. (2005). *External knowledge: A review of the literature addressing the role of external knowledge and expertise at key stages of business growth and development*. Advanced Institute of Management.

Bhide, A. V. (2003). *The origin and evolution of new businesses*. Oxford University Press.

Bhuiyan, M. B. U., & Nguyen, T. H. T. (2019). "Impact of ESG disclosures on firm performance: The mediating role of loan costs". *Journal of Financial Economics*.

Bibeault, D. B. (1999). *Corporate Turnaround. How Managers Turn Losers into Winners*. Washington: Beard.

Bloomberg. (2022). *U. S. convertible bond market data*. Retrieved from Bloomberg.

BMWI. (2021). *Gross value added by sector in Germany, 2017*. https://www.bmwi.de/Redaktion/EN/Infografiken/gross-value-addes-by-sector.html

Bonate, P. L. (2011). *Pharmacokinetic-pharmacodynamic modeling and simulation* (2nd ed.). Springer.

Booth, L., Aivazian, V., Demirguc-Kunt, A., & Maksimovic, V. (2001). Capital structures in developing countries. *The Journal of Finance*, *56*(1), 87–130.

Bortz, J., & Schuster, C. (2010). Statistik für Human- und Sozialwissenschaftler (7th ed.). Berlin: Springer.

Börner, C., Grichnik, D., & Reize, F. (2010). Finanzierungsentscheidungen mittelständischer Unternehmer – Einflussfaktoren der Fremdfinanzierung deutscher KMU. *Schmalenbachs Zeitschrift für betriebswirtschaftliche Forschung*, *62*(2), 227–275. https://doi.org/10.1007/BF03377359.

Bottazzi, G., & Secchi, A. (2003). Why are distributions of firm growth rates tent-shaped? *Economics Letters*, *80*(3), 415–420.

Bradley, M., Jarrell, G. A., & Kim, E. H. (1984). On the existence of an optimal capital structure: Theory and evidence. *The Journal of Finance*, *39*(3), 857–878.

Braun, V., Clarke, V., Hayfield, N., & Terry, G. (2017). Thematic analysis. In P. Liamputtong (Ed.), *Handbook of research methods in health social sciences* (pp. 843–860). Springer Singapore.

Breckinridge Capital Advisors. (2024). *Q2 2024 corporate bond market outlook*. www.breckinridge.com/insights/details/q2-2024-corporate-bond-market-outlook/

Brennan, M. J., & Schwartz, E. S. (1978). Corporate income taxes, valuation, and the problem of optimal capital structure. *The Journal of Business*, *51*(1), 103–114.

Brennan, M. J., & Schwartz, E. S. (1984). Optimal Financial Policy and Firm Valuation. *The Journal of Finance*, *39*(3), 593–607. https://doi.org/10.2307/2327917

Bromiley, P. (1991). Testing a Causal Model of Corporate Risk Taking and Performance. *Academy of Management Journal*, *34*(1), 37–59. https://doi.org/10.5465/256301

Brost, H. (Ed.). (2005). *Unternehmensnachfolge im Mittelstand*. 2nd Edition. Bankakademie-Verlag.

Bruner, R. F., Eades, K. M., Harris, R. S., & Higgins, R. C. (1998). Best practices in estimating the cost of capital: Survey and synthesis. *Financial Practice and Education*, *8*(1), 13–28.

Brusov, P., Filatova, T., & Orekhova, N. (2022). *Generalized Modigliani – Miller theory: Applications in corporate finance, investments, taxation, and ratings*. Springer International Publishing.

Bryman, A., & Bell, E. (2011). *Business research methods* (3rd ed.). Oxford University Press.

Bulut, C., & Can, O. (2013). Business performance. In *Encyclopedia of corporate social responsibility* (pp. 273–279). Springer.

Burke, R. J. (2002). *Organizational change: Theory and practice*. Sage Publications.

Buschmann, H. (2006). *Erfolgreiches Turnaround-Management. Empirische Untersuchung mit Schwerpunkt auf den Einfluss der Stakeholder*. Wiesbaden: Gabler Springer.

Buzzell, R. D., Gale, B. T., & Sultan, R. G. (1975). *Market share: a key to profitability. Harvard Business Review*, *53*(1), 97–106.

Buzzell, R. D., & Gale, B. T. (1989). *The PIMS principles: Linking strategy to performance*. Free Press.

Campbell, J. Y., Lo, A. W., & MacKinlay, A. C. (1997). *The econometrics of financial markets*. Princeton University Press.

Campello, M., Graham, J. R., & Harvey, C. R. (2010). The real effects of financial constraints: Evidence from a financial crisis. *Journal of Financial Economics*, *97*(3), 470–487.

Castrogiovannia, G. J., & Bruton, G. D. (2000). Business Turnaround Processes Following Acquisitions: Reconsidering the Role of Retrenchment, *Journal of Business Research*, *48*(1), 25–34.

Chadha, S., & Sharma, A. K. (2015). Capital Structure and Firm Performance: Empirical Evidence from India. *Vision*, *19*(4), 295–302. https://doi.org/10.1177/0972262915610852

Chaganti, R., Cook, R. G., & Smeltz, W. J. (2002). Effects of styles, strategies, and systems on the growth of small businesses. *Journal of Developmental Entrepreneurship, 7*(2), 175.

Chen, J. J. (2004). Determinants of capital structure of Chinese-listed companies. *Journal of Business Research, 57*(12), 1341–1351.

China Banking and Insurance Regulatory Commission [CBIRC]. (2022). *Annual report.* Retrieved from CBIRC.

China Leasing Alliance. (2022). *Annual Leasing Report.*

China Three Gorges. (2022). *Annual report.* China Three Gorges Corporation.

China Venture. (2022). *Investment statistics.* Retrieved from China Venture.

Churchill, N. C., & Lewis, V. L. (1983). The five stages of small business growth. *Harvard Business Review, 61*(3), 30–50. https://hbr.org/1983/05/the-five-stages-of-small-business-growth

Claessens, S., & Laeven, L. (2003). Financial development, property rights, and growth. *The Journal of Finance, 58*(6), 2401–2436.

Clark, G. L., Feiner, A., & Viehs, M. (2015). From the Stockholder to the Stakeholder: How Sustainability Can Drive Financial Outperformance.

Cleves, M. A., Gould, W. W., Gutierrez, R. G., & Marchenko, Y. V. (2010). *An introduction to survival analysis using Stata* (3rd ed.). Stata Press.

Climate Bonds Initiative. (2020). *Green bonds market summary.* Climate Bonds Initiative.

Climate Bonds Initiative. (2022). *Sustainable debt market summary H1 2022.* www.climatebonds.net/

Coad, A., & Rao, R. (2010). Firm Growth and R&D expenditure. *Economics of Innovation and New Technology, 19*(2), 127–145.

Coad, A., Cowling, M., Nightingale, P., Pellegrino, G., Savona, M., & Siepel, J. (2014). *Innovative Firms and Growth.* London: Macmillan.

Coase, R. H. (1937). The Nature of the Firm. *Economica, 4*(16), 386–405. https://doi.org/10.2307/2626876

Coleman, S. (2000). Access to capital and terms of credit: A comparison of men- and women-owned small businesses. *Journal of Small Business Management, 38*, 37–52.

Crowdfund Insider. (2022). *StartEngine raised $189 million in 2022, considering more acquisitions.* www.crowdfundinsider.com

Dalley, J., & Hamilton, B. (2000). Knowledge, context and learning in the small business. *International Small Business Journal, 18*(3), 51–59.

Damodaran, A. (2002). *Investment Valuation: Tools and Techniques.* New York: Wiley.

Davidsson, P., Delmar, F., & Wiklund, J. (2002). Entrepreneurship as growth: Growth as entrepreneurship. In M. A. Hitt, R. D. Ireland, S. M. Camp, & D. L. Sexton (Eds.), *Strategic entrepreneurship: Creating a new mindset.* Blackwell Publishers.

Daunfeldt, S., Elert, N. & Johansson, D. (2010). *The economic contribution of high-growth firms: Do definitions matter? HUI* Working Papers, No 35.

Davidsson, P., & Delmar. (2006). High-Growth Firms and Their Contribution To Employment: The Case Of Sweden 1987–96. In P.

Davidsson, F. Delmar, J. Wiklund & P. Davidsson (eds.), *Entrepreneurship and the Growth of Firms* (pp. 156–178). Cheltenham: Edward Elgar.

Davis, M. (2015). Solving the problem of survivorship bias in hedge fund indices. *Journal of Alternative Investments, 18*(1), 62–83.

Deakins, D., & Freel, M. (1998). Entrepreneurial learning and the growth process in SMEs. *The Learning Organization, 5*(3), 144–155.

Dealogic. (2022). *Preferred securities market data.* https://dealogic.com/

Delmar, F., Davidsson, P., & Gartner, W. B. (2003). Arriving at the high-growth firm. *Journal of Business Venturing, 18*(2), 189–216.

Deloitte China. (2022). *2022 Review and 2023 Outlook for Chinese Mainland & HK IPO markets.* Retrieved from Deloitte China.

Demirgüç-Kunt, A., & Maksimovic, V. (1998). Law, finance, and firm growth. *The Journal of Finance, 53*(6), 2107–2137.

Denis, D. J., & Mihov, V. T. (2003). The choice among bank debt, non-bank private debt, and public debt: Evidence from new corporate borrowings. *Journal of Financial Economics, 70*(1), 3–28.

Dobbs, M., & Hamilton, R. T. (2007). Small business growth: Recent evidence and new directions. *International Journal of Entrepreneurial Behavior & Research, 13*(5), 296–322.

Doukas, J. A., Guo, J., & Zhou, B. (2011). Hot IPO markets and the long-run underperformance of IPOs. *Journal of Banking & Finance, 35*(3), 821–838.

Drucker, P. (1954). *The practice of management.* Harper & Row.

Duttagupta, R., & Pazarbasioglu, C. (2021). *Miles to go.* Finance & Development, International Monetary Fund.

Dwivedi, D. N. (2010). *Managerial economics* (8th ed.). Vikas Publishing House.

Easterby-Smith, M., Thorpe, R., & Jackson, P. R. (2015). *Management and business research* (5th ed.). Sage Publications.

Eccles, R. G., Ioannou, I., & Serafeim, G. (2014). The impact of corporate sustainability on organizational processes and performance. *Management Science, 60*(11), 2835–2857.

Eccles, R. G., Ioannou, I., & Serafeim, G. (2019). The comprehensive business case for sustainability. *Harvard Business Review, 97*(5), 100–109.

Eichhorn, P., & Gleißner, W. (2016). *Produktions- und Kostentheorie.* Gabler Verlag.

Eichner, T. (2010). *Restructuring and Turnaround of Distressed Manufacturing Firms.* An International Empirical Study. Frankfurt: Lang.

Eriotis, N. P., Frangouli, Z., & Ventoura-Neokosmides, Z. (2002). Profit Margin And Capital Structure: An Empirical Relationship. *Journal of Applied Business Research (JABR), 18*(2), Article 2. https://doi.org/10.19030/jabr.v18i2.2118

Euronext. (2022). *Euronext confirms its position as the leading equity listing venue in Europe and debt listing worldwide in 2022.* Retrieved from Euronext.

European Central Bank. (2022a). *Sector accounts.* www.ecb.europa.eu/stats/sectaccounts/html/index.en.html

European Central Bank. (2022b). *Survey on the Access to Finance of Enterprises: Tighter financing conditions and an expected deterioration in the economic environment.* Retrieved from ECB.

European Commission. (2020a). *EU taxonomy for sustainable activities.* European Commission.

European Commission. (2020b). *MiFID II and CRD IV regulations.* Retrieved from European Commission.

European Investment Fund. (2022). *EIF for venture capital & private equity funds.* Retrieved from EIF.

European Payment Report. (2022). *Economic analysis.* Intrum UK.

Evans, D. S. (1987). Tests of alternative theories of firm growth. *Journal of Political Economy, 95*(4), 657–674.

EY. (2023). *Global FinTech adoption index 2023.* Ernst & Young.

Fadahunsi, A. (2012). The growth of small businesses: Towards a research agenda. *American Journal of Economics and Business Administration, 4*(1), 105–115.

Fama, E. F. (1970). Efficient capital markets: A review of theory and empirical work. *The Journal of Finance, 25*(2), 383–417.

Fama, E. F. (1980). Agency Problems and the Theory of the Firm. *Journal of Political Economy, 88*(2), 288–307.

Fama, E. F., & French, K. R. (2002). Testing trade-off and pecking order predictions about dividends and debt. *The Review of Financial Studies, 15*(1), 1–33.

Fama, E. F., & French, K. R. (2005). Financing decisions: Who issues stock? *Journal of Financial Economics, 76*(3), 549–582. https://doi.org/10.1016/j.jfineco.2004.10.003

Faulkender, M., & Petersen, M. A. (2006). Does the source of capital affect capital structure? *The Review of Financial Studies, 19*(1), 45–79.

Federal Reserve (2022). Financial Accounts of the United States.

Federal Reserve Bank of St. Louis. (2024). https://fred.stlouisfed.org/series/AAA

Finch, N. (2002). *Corporate finance: Concepts and strategies.* Pearson Education Australia.

Flammer, C. (2021). Green bonds: Effectiveness and implications for public policy. *Environmental and Energy Policy and the Economy*, 2, 95–128.

Fortune Business Insights. (2024). *Fintech market size, share & industry analysis.* By Technology (API, AI, Blockchain, Distributed Computing), by Application (Payments, Fund Transfer, Personal Finance, Loans, Insurance, Wealth Management), by End User (BFSI, Retail & Ecommerce, Healthcare, Trading, Government) and Regional Forecast 2023–2028.

Fosu, S. (2013). Capital structure, product market competition and firm performance: Evidence from South Africa. *The Quarterly Review of Economics and Finance, 53*(2), 140–151. https://doi.org/10.1016/j.qref.2013.02.004

Frank, M. Z., & Goyal, V. K. (2003). Testing the pecking order theory of capital structure. *Journal of Financial Economics, 67*(2), 217–248. https://doi.org/10.1016/S0304-405X(02)00252-0

Frank, M. Z., & Goyal, V. K. (2009). Capital structure decisions: Which factors are reliably important? *Financial Management*, *38*(1), 1–37. https://doi.org/10.1111/j.1755-053X.2009.01026.x.

Frank, M. Z., & Goyal, V. K. (2015). Trade-off and pecking order theories of debt. In R. A. Harris, S. N. Kaplan, & M. S. Weisbach (Eds.), *Handbook of the economics of finance* (Vol. 2, pp. 135–202). Elsevier.

Freel, M. S., & Robson, P. J. A. (2004). Small firm innovation, growth and performance: Evidence from Scotland and Northern England. *International Small Business Journal*, *22*(6), 561–575.

Frenz, M., & Letto-Gilles, G. (2009). The impact on innovation performance of different sources of knowledge: Evidence from the UK community innovation survey. *Research Policy*, *38*(7), 1125–1135.

Friede, G., Busch, T., & Bassen, A. (2015). ESG and financial performance: Aggregated evidence from more than 2000 empirical studies. *Journal of Sustainable Finance & Investment*, *5*(4), 210–233.

Frydenberg, S. (2004). Theory of capital structure – A review. *The Journal of Finance*, *49*(1), 148–160.

Gao, H., Harford, J., & Li, K. (2013). Determinants of corporate cash policy: Insights from private firms. *Journal of Financial Economics*, *109*(3), 623–639. https://doi.org/10.1016/j.jfineco.2013.04.008

GE annual report. (2022). General Electric Company. https://www.ge.com/news/reports/ge-releases-2022-annual-report

Gellweiler, C. (2018). Cohesion of RBV and industry view for competitive positioning. *Strategic Management*, *23*(2), 3–12.

Gibrat, R. (1931). *Les Inégalités Économiques*. Librairie du Recueil Sirey.

Giese, G., Lee, L. E., Melas, D., Nagy, Z., & Nishikawa, L. (2019). Foundations of ESG investing: How ESG affects equity valuation, risk, and performance. *The Journal of Portfolio Management*, *45*(5), 69–83.

Ginter, P. M., Duncan, W. J., & Swayne, L. E. (2018). *Strategic management of health care organizations* (8th ed.). Wiley.

Goddard, J., Tavakoli, M., & Wilson, J. O. S. (2005). Determinants of profitability in European manufacturing and services: Evidence from a dynamic panel model. *Applied Financial Economics*, *15*(18), 1269–1282. https://doi.org/10.1080/09603100500387139

Gompers, P. A., & Lerner, J. (2022). *The venture capital cycle*. MIT Press.

González, V. M. (2013). Leverage and corporate performance: International evidence. *International Review of Economics & Finance*, *25*, 169–184. https://doi.org/10.1016/j.iref.2012.07.005

Gordon, M. J. (1992). The neoclassical and a post Keynesian theory of investment. *Journal of Post Keynesian Economics*, *14*(4), 425–443.

Graham, J. R., & Harvey, C. R. (1997). Market timing ability and volatility implied in investment newsletters' asset allocation recommendations. *Journal of Financial Economics*, *42*(3), 397–421.

Graham, J. R., & Harvey, C. R. (2001). The theory and practice of corporate finance: Evidence from the field. *Journal of Financial Economics*, *60*(2–3), 187–243.

Graham, J. R., & Leary, M. T. (2011). A review of empirical capital structure research and directions for the future. *Annual Review of Financial Economics*, *3*(1), 309–345.

Graham, J. R., Harvey, C. R., & Puri, M. (2013). Managerial attitudes and corporate actions. *Journal of Financial Economics, 109*(1), 103–121. https://doi.org/10.1016/j.jfineco.2013.01.010

Graham, J. R., Leary, M. T., & Roberts, M. R. (2015). A century of capital structure: The leveraging of corporate America. *Journal of Financial Economics, 118*(3), 658–683.

Greiner, L. E. (1972). Evolution and revolution as organizations grow. *Harvard Business Review, 76.*

Greiner, L. E. (1998). Evolution and revolution as organizations grow. *Harvard Business Review, 76*(3), 55–68.

Grinyer, P. H., & Mayes, D. G., & McKiernan, P. (1988). *Sharpbenders. The Secrets of Unleashing Corporate Potential.* Oxford: Oxford University Press.

Gropp, R., & Heider, F. (2008). *The determinants of capital structure: Some evidence from banks* [Working Paper]. http://ub-madoc.bib.uni-mannheim.de/1918.

Gruenwald, H. (2016). *Unternehmenswachstum und strategisches Management.* Springer Gabler.

Habib, A., Uddin Bhuiyan, B., & Islam, A. (2013). Financial distress, earnings management and market pricing of accruals during the global financial crisis. *Managerial Finance, 39*(2), 155–180. https://doi.org/10.1108/03074351311294007

Hackbarth, D. (2008). Managerial traits and capital structure decisions. *Journal of Financial and Quantitative Analysis, 43*(4), 843–881.

Hair, J. F., Black, W. C., Babin, B. J., & Anderson, R. E. (2014). *Multivariate data analysis* (7th ed.). Pearson.

Hall, G., Hutchinson, P., & Michaelas, N. (2000). Industry effects on the determinants of unquoted SMEs' capital structure. *International Journal of the Economics of Business, 7*(3), 297–312. https://doi.org/10.1080/13571510050197203.

Hall, R. E., & Lieberman, M. (2012). *Microeconomics: Principles and Applications.* Cengage Learning.

Hall, R. E., & Lieberman, M. (2013). *Economics: Principles and applications.* Cengage Learning.

Hamel, G., & Prahalad, C. K. (1990). The Core Competence of the Corporation. *Harvard Business Review, 68*(3), 79–90.

Hamel, G., & Prahalad, C. K. (1994). Competing for the future. *Harvard Business Review, 72.*

Harris, M., & Raviv, A. (1991). The theory of capital structure. *The Journal of Finance, 46*(1), 297–355.

Hartmann, S. (2016). *Turnaround-Management im deutschsprachigen Raum: Empirische Studie zum Turnaround und Lebenszyklus in Deutschland, der Schweiz und Österreich.* Göttingen: Cuvillier.

Havlik, P., & Stehrer, R. (2012). European industry in international comparison. In J. B. Weiss (Ed.), *European competitiveness report 2012* (pp. 89–111). European Union.

Helfrich, H. (2016). *Wissenschaftstheorie für Betriebswirtschaftler.* Springer Fachmedien.

Helwege, J., & Liang, N. (2004). Initial public offerings in hot and cold markets. *Journal of Financial and Quantitative Analysis, 39*(3), 541–569.

Henrekson, M., & Johansson, D. (2010). Gazelles as Job Creators. *Small Business Economics, 35*, 227–244.

Hens, T., & Pamini, P. (2008). *Grundzüge der analytischen Mikroökonomie*. Springer Berlin Heidelberg. https://doi.org/10.1007/978-3-540-28158-0

Herr, C. (2007). *Nicht-lineare Wirkungsbeziehungen von Erfolgsfaktoren der Unternehmensgründung*. Wiesbaden: DVU/GWV.

High-Level Expert Group on Sustainable Finance (HLEG). (2018). Financing a Sustainable European Economy.

Hirschey, M. (2008). *Fundamentals of Managerial Economics* (9th ed.). Cengage Learning.

Hoffmann-Burchardi, U. (2001). Clustering of initial public offerings, information revelation and underpricing. *European Economic Review, 45*(2), 353–383.

Holtmann, C. (2010). Stepwise regression analysis: A model selection tool. In P. J. Patel (Ed.), *Regression analysis* (pp. 101–120). InTech.

Hölzl, W. (2009). Is the R&D Behaviour of Fast-Growing SMEs different? *Small Business Economics, 1*, 59–75.

Howorth, C., & Westhead, P. (2003). The focus of working capital management in UK small firms. *Management Accounting Research, 14*, 94–111.

Hsu, S., Li, M., & Tsai, K. (2019). *Financial development and innovation in China*. Edward Elgar Publishing.

Huang, R., & Ritter, J. R. (2009). Testing theories of capital structure and estimating the speed of adjustment. *Journal of Financial and Quantitative Analysis, 44*(2), 237–271.

Institute for Supply Management. (2022). *Spring and fall semiannual economic forecasts*. Economic Report. www.ismworld.org/

Intrum. (2022). *European payment report 2022*. Retrieved from Intrum.

Invest Europe. (2022). *Investing in Europe: Private equity activity 2022*. Retrieved from Invest Europe.

Iyoha, F. O., & Umoru, D. (2017). An empirical analysis of the impact of corporate taxation on investment in Nigeria. *Journal of Business and Management, 19*(1), 56–64.

Jensen, M. C. (1986). Agency costs of free cash flow, corporate finance, and takeovers. *The American Economic Review, 76*(2), 323–329.

Jensen, M. C., & Meckling, W. H. (1976). Theory of the firm: Managerial behavior, agency costs, and ownership structure. *Journal of Financial Economics, 3*(4), 305–360.

Jiang, Z., & Lie, E. (2016). Cash holding adjustments and managerial entrenchment. *Journal of Corporate Finance, 36*, 190–205. https://doi.org/10.1016/j.jcorpfin.2015.12.008

Kahneman, D., & Lovallo, D. (1993). Timid Choices and Bold Forecasts: A Cognitive Perspective on Risk Taking. *Management Science, 39*(1), 17–31.

Kaldasch, J. (2012). Evolutionary model of the growth and size of firms. *Physica A: Statistical Mechanics and its Applications*, *391*(14), 3751–3769.

Kane, G. D., & Richardson, F. M. (2002). The Relationship between Changes in Fixed Plant Investment and the Likelihood of Emergence from Corporate Financial Distress. *Review of Quantitative Finance and Accounting*, *18*(3), 259–272.

Kanji, G. K., Malek, A., & Tambi, B. A. (2015). Total quality management and business excellence. *Total Quality Management*, *6*(3), 67–75.

Kaserer, C. (2013). *Auswirkung der CRD IV (Basel III) auf die Unternehmensfinanzierung*. Vereinigung der Bayerischen Wirtschaft.

Katsamitros, G. (2019). Analyzing the decline in listed companies. In K. Warren (Ed.), *Financial markets* (pp. 159–176). Routledge.

Kebewar, M. (2013). The effect of Debt on Corporate Profitability: Evidence from French Service Sector. *Brussels Economic Review*, *56*(1), 43–59.

Knudsen, T., Levinthal, D. A., & Winter, S. G. (2017). Systematic differences and random rates: Reconciling Gibrat's law with firm differences. *Strategy Science*, *2*(2), 111–120.

Kordanuli, B., Barjaktarović, L., Jeremić, L., & Alizamir, M. (2017). Appraisal of artificial neural network for forecasting of economic parameters. *Physica A: Statistical Mechanics and Its Applications*, *465*, 515–519. https://doi.org/10.1016/j.physa.2016.08.062

Koski, H., & Pajarinen, M. (2011). The role of business subsidies in job creation of start-ups, gazelles and incumbents. *Small Business Economics*, *36*(4), 503–529.

Kotler, P. (1999). *Kotler on marketing: How to create, win, and dominate markets*. Free Press.

Kraus, A., & Litzenberger, R. H. (1973). A state-preference model of optimal financial leverage. *The Journal of Finance*, *28*(4), 911–922.

Kuč, V., & Kaličanin, Đ. (2021). Determinants of the capital structure of large companies: Evidence from Serbia. *Economic Research-Ekonomska Istraživanja*, *34*(1), 590–607. https://doi.org/10.1080/1331677X.2020.1801484

Kuehnhausen, F., & Stieber, H. W. (2014). Determinants of Capital Structure in Non-Financial Companies. *SSRN Electronic Journal*, 1–57. https://doi.org/10.2139/ssrn.2410741

Kutner, M. H., Nachtsheim, C. J., Neter, J., & Li, W. (2005). *Applied linear statistical models* (5th ed.). McGraw-Hill Irwin.

La Porta, R., Lopez-de-Silanes, F., Shleifer, A., & Vishny, R. W. (1998). Law and finance. *Journal of Political Economy*, *106*(6), 1113–1155.

Lambert, T., & Schwienbacher, A. (2010). *An empirical analysis of crowdfunding*. Social Science Research Network.

Lamont, O. (1997). Cash flow and investment: Evidence from internal capital markets. *Journal of Finance*, *52*(1), 83–109.

Lawrimore, E. (2011). The new performance challenge. *Performance Improvement*, *50*(3), 5–12.

Leary, M. T. (2009). Bank Loan Supply, Lender Choice, and Corporate Capital Structure. *The Journal of Finance*, *64*(3), 1143–1185. https://doi.org/10.1111/j.1540-6261.2009.01461.x

Leary, M. T., & Roberts, M. R. (2010). The pecking order, debt capacity, and information asymmetry. *Journal of Financial Economics, 95*(3), 332–355. https://doi.org/10.1016/j.jfineco.2009.10.009

Leaseurope. (2022). *Leaseurope annual review of 2022.* Retrieved from Leaseurope.

Leland, H. E. (1994). Corporate debt value, bond covenants, and optimal capital structure. *The Journal of Finance*, *49*(4), 1213–1252.

Lemmon, M. L., Roberts, M. R., & Zender, J. F. (2008). Back to the Beginning: Persistence and the Cross-Section of Corporate Capital Structure. *The Journal of Finance, 63*(4), 1575–1608. https://doi.org/10.1111/j.1540-6261.2008.01369.x

Lemmon, M. L., & Roberts, M. R. (2010). The Response of Corporate Financing and Investment to Changes in the Supply of Credit. *Journal of Financial and Quantitative Analysis, 45*(3), 555–587. Cambridge Core. https://doi.org/10.1017/S0022109010000256

Lemmon, M. L., & Zender, J. F. (2010). Debt Capacity and Tests of Capital Structure Theories. *Journal of Financial and Quantitative Analysis, 45*(5), 1161–1187. Cambridge Core. https://doi.org/10.1017/S0022109010000499

Li, Y., Liu, Y., & Ren, F. (2019). Exploring the effect of firm characteristics on the relationship between TMT characteristics and firm performance. *International Journal of Business and Management*, *14*(3), 130–145.

Linklaters. (2024). "ESG Legal Outlook 2024: Key themes in Europe". Linklaters.

Lippmann, R. P. (1987). An introduction to computing with neural networks. *IEEE ASSP Magazine*, *4*(2), 4–22.

Liu, X., Xiao, W., & Yuan, J. (2019). *Understanding Guanxi in China: Management, culture, and business practice.* Routledge.

Loos, N. (2006). *Value creation in leveraged buyouts.* DUV.

López-Garcia, P., & Puente, S. (2009). What makes a high-growth firm? A clustering analysis of Spanish gazelles. *Small Business Economics*, *32*(4), 415–428.

Lozano, M. B., & Durán, J. J. (2017). Family firm and capital structure: The role of the board of directors. *Corporate Governance: An International Review*, *25*(4), 236–253.

Luo, Y., & Jiang, C. (2022). The impact of corporate capital structure on financial performance based on convolutional neural network. *Computational Intelligence and Neuroscience*, *2022*, e5895560.

Ma, H. (2000). Competitive advantage and firm performance. *Competitiveness Review: An International Business Journal*, *10*(2), 15–32. https://doi.org/10.1108/eb046396

Mac an Bhaird, C. (2010). *Resourcing small and medium sized enterprises.* Springer.

Malik, F. (2008). *Ende des Blindflugs mit PIMS.* M.O.M.

Malmendier, U., Tate, G., & Yan, J. (2011). Overconfidence and early-life experiences: The effect of managerial traits on corporate financial policies. *The Journal of Finance*, *66*(5), 1687–1733.

Margaritis, D., & Psillaki, M. (2010). Capital structure, equity ownership and firm performance. *Journal of Banking & Finance*, *34*(3), 621–632.

Market Data Forecast. (2024). *Fintech market size, share, trends and forecast 2024–2029.* https://www.marketdataforecast.com/market-reports/fintech-market
Masulis, R. W. (1983). The impact of capital structure change on firm value: Some estimates. *The Journal of Finance*, *38*(1), 107–126.
Maury, B. (2006). Family ownership and firm performance: Empirical evidence from western European corporations. *Journal of Corporate Finance*, *12*(2), 321–341.
McKinsey & Company. (2020). *Valuing sustainability in the boardroom.* McKinsey Quarterly.
McMenamin, J. (1999). *Financial management: An introduction.* Routledge.
Mertler, C. A., & Reinhart, R. A. (2017). *Advanced and multivariate statistical methods: Practical application and interpretation* (6th ed.). Routledge.
Meyer, C. A. (2007). *Working Capital und Unternehmenswert. Eine Analyse zum Management der Forderungen und Verbindlichkeiten aus Lieferungen und Leistungen*. Wiesbaden: Gabler Springer.
Miller, C. C., Washburn, N. T., & Glick, W. H. (2013). Perspective – The myth of firm performance. *Organization Science*, *24*(3), 948–964. https://doi.org/10.1287/orsc.1120.0762
Miller, M. H., & Rock, K. (1985). Dividend policy under asymmetric information. *The Journal of Finance*, *40*(4), 1031–1051.
Milosevic, I., & Bass, A. E. (2017). When there were none: Discovering the origins of dynamic capabilities in a high-growth firm. *Academy of Management Proceedings*, *2017*, 10572.
Modigliani, F., & Miller, M. H. (1958). The cost of capital, corporation finance and the theory of investment. *The American Economic Review*, *48*(3), 261–297.
Modigliani, F., & Miller, M. H. (1963). Corporate income taxes and the cost of capital: A correction. *The American Economic Review*, *53*(3), 433–443.
Mollick, E. (2014). The dynamics of crowdfunding: An exploratory study. *Journal of Business Venturing*, *29*(1), 1–16.
Mordor Intelligence. (2024). *Fintech market – growth, trends, COVID-19 impact, and forecasts (2024–2029).* https://www.mordorintelligence.com/industry-reports/global-fintech-market
Morrow, J. L., Johnson, R. A., & Busenitz, L. W. (2004). The Effects of Cost and Asset Retrenchment on Firm Performance: The Overlooked Role of a Firm's Competitive Environment. *Journal of Management*, *30*(2), 189–208.
Most, K. S. (1977). *Accounting theory*. University of Virginia.
Mowen, M. M., Hansen, D. R., & Heitger, D. L. (2018). *Managerial Accounting: The Cornerstone of Business Decision-Making*. Cengage Learning.
Mueller, S. L. (2007). Assessing the effectiveness of entrepreneurship education programs: A comparative study. *Journal of Small Business Management*, *45*(4), 429–446.

Muhammad, H., Shah, B., & Islam, Z. ul. (2014). The Impact of Capital Structure on Firm Performance: Evidence from Pakistan. *The Journal of Industrial Distribution & Business*, *5*(2), 13–20. https://doi.org/10.13106/jidb.2014.vol5.no2.13

Müller, H. E. (2013). *Unternehmensführung: Strategien, Konzepte, Praxisbeispiele*. Munich: Oldenbourg.

Mwambuli, E. L. (2016). Does corporate capital structure influence corporate financial performance in developing economies? Evidence from East African stock markets. *International Finance and Banking*, *3*(1), 97–123.

Myers, S. C. (1977). Determinants of corporate borrowing. *Journal of Financial Economics*, *5*(2), 147–175.

Myers, S. C. (1984). The capital structure puzzle. *The Journal of Finance*, *39*(3), 574–592.

Myers, S. C., & Majluf, N. S. (1984). Corporate financing and investment decisions when firms have information that investors do not have. *Journal of Financial Economics*, *13*(2), 187–221.

Myers, S. C. (2003). Chapter 4—Financing of Corporations. In G. M. Constantinides, M. Harris, & R. M. Stulz (Eds.), *Handbook of the Economics of Finance* (Vol. 1, pp. 215–253). Elsevier. https://doi.org/10.1016/S1574-0102(03)01008-2

Napier, C. J. (2009). Historiography. In J. R. Edwards & S. P. Walker (Eds.), *The Routledge companion to accounting history* (pp. 30–49). Routledge.

NASDAQ. (2022). *Annual IPO statistics*. https://ir.nasdaq.com/news-releases/news-release-details/nasdaq-welcomes-156-ipos-and-29-exchange-transfers-2022

National Venture Capital Association (2022). Yearbook.

Naughton, B. (2018). *The Chinese economy: Adaptation and growth*. MIT Press.

Naujoks, M. B. (2012). *Restructuring Strategies and Post-Bankruptcy Performance* (PhD Thesis). Munich: Technical University of Munich.

Negishi, T. (2014). Microeconomic Foundations of Macroeconomics. In *Elements of Neo-Walrasian Economics* (pp. 167–184). Springer.

Nguyen, T. D. K., & Ramachandran, N. (2006). Capital Structure in Small and Medium-sized Enterprises: The Case of Vietnam. *ASEAN Economic Bulletin*, *23*(2), 192–211.

Nothardt, F. (2001). *Corporate Turnaround and Corporate Stakeholders: An Empirical Examination of the Determinants of Corporate Turnaround in Germany with Focus on Financial Stakeholder Theory* (PhD Thesis). St. Gallen: University of St. Gallen.

Nunes, P. J. M., Serrasqueiro, Z. M., & Sequeira, T. N. (2009). Profitability in Portuguese service industries: A panel data approach. *The Service Industries Journal*, *29*(5), 693–707. https://doi.org/10.1080/02642060902720188

OECD. (2010). *High-growth enterprises: What governments can do to make a difference*. OECD Studies on SMEs and Entrepreneurship. OECD Publishing.

OECD. (2015). *Measuring and managing ESG risks in pension funds.* OECD Publishing.

OECD. (2022). *Blockchain and the future of finance.* OECD Publishing.

Ogebe, P., Ogebe, J., & Alewi, K. (2013, March 27). *The impact of capital structure on firms' performance in Nigeria* [MPRA Paper].

Olson, P. D., & Bokor, D. W. (1995). Strategy process-content interaction: Effects on growth performance in small, start-up firms. *Journal of Small Business Management, 33*(1), 1–34.

Palepu, K. G., Healy, P. M. & Peek, E. (2007). *Business Analysis and Valuation (IFRS Edition).* London: Thomson.

Pant, L. W. (1991). An Investigation of Industry and Firm Structural Characteristics in Corporate Turnarounds. *Journal of Management Studies, 28*(6), 623–643.

Pao, H.-T. (2008). A comparison of neural network and multiple regression analysis in modeling capital structure. *Expert Systems with Applications, 35*(3), 720–727.

Pedhazur, E. J. (1997). *Multiple regression in behavioral research: Explanation and prediction* (3rd ed.). Wadsworth.

Penrose, E. (1959). *The theory of the growth of the firm.* Basil Blackwell.

People's Bank of China. (2022). *Financial statistics report.* Retrieved from PBOC.

Phelps, R., Adams, R., & Bessant, J. (2007). Life cycles of growing organizations: A review with implications for knowledge and learning. *International Journal of Management Reviews, 9*(1), 1–30.

Pijourlet, G. (2013). "The impact of CSR on capital structure decisions". *Journal of Business Ethics.*

PitchBook. (2022). *Venture capital report.* PitchBook Data, Inc.

Porter, M. E. (1980). *Competitive strategy: Techniques for analyzing industries and competitors.* Free Press.

Porter, M. E. (1991). Towards a dynamic theory of strategy. *Strategic Management Journal, 12*(S2), 95–117.

Porter, M. E. (1996). What is strategy? *Harvard Business Review, 74*(6), 61–78.

Porter, M. E. (2008). The Five Competitive Forces That Shape Strategy. *Harvard Business Review, 86*(1), pp. 79–93.

Porter, M. E., & Kramer, M. R. (2011). Creating shared value. *Harvard Business Review, 89*(1/2), 62–77.

Preqin. (2022a). *Preqin global private equity & venture capital report.* Retrieved from Preqin.

Preqin. (2022b). *Private credit demonstrates resiliency amid current economic conditions.* www.adamsstreetpartners.com/

Prittwitz, U. v. (2022). Economic and political implications of climate change. In G. Winter (Ed.), *Climate change and environmental law* (pp. 145–162). Edward Elgar Publishing.

Psillaki, M., & Daskalakis, N. (2009). Are the determinants of capital structure country or firm specific? *Small Business Economics, 33*(3), 319–333. https://doi.org/10.1007/s11187-008-9103-4

PwC China. (2022). *Global IPO watch 2022.* www.pwc.com/gx/en/services/audit-assurance/assets/pwc-global-ipo-watch-2022.pdf

Quon, T. K., Zeghal, D., & Maingot, M. (2012). Enterprise risk management and business performance during the financial and economic crises. *Problems and Perspectives in Management, 10*(3), 95–103.

Rajan, R. G., & Zingales, L. (1995). What do we know about capital structure? Some evidence from international data. *The Journal of Finance, 50*(5), 1421–1460.

Ramachandra, V. S., & Nageswara Rao, S. V. D. (2008). *Capital Structure, Industry Pricing, and Firm Performance* (SSRN Scholarly Paper No. 1263245). Social Science Research Network. https://doi.org/10.2139/ssrn.1263245

Ramanujam, V. (1984). Research on corporate diversification: A synthesis. *Strategic Management Journal, 5*(3), 299–319.

Rao, N. V., Al-Yahyaee, K. H. M., & Syed, L. A. (2007). Capital structure and financial performance: Evidence from Oman. *Indian Journal of Economics and Business, 6*(1), 1–14.

Rau, P. R. (2008). The Empirical Evidence on Mergers. In C. Krishnamurti & S. R. Vishwanath (Eds.), *Mergers, Acquisitions and Corporate Restructuring* (pp. 212–247). Thousand Oaks: SAGE.

Rauh, J. D., & Sufi, A. (2010). Capital Structure and Debt Structure. *The Review of Financial Studies, 23*(12), 4242–4280. https://doi.org/10.1093/rfs/hhq095

Reichstein, T., & Dahl, M. S. (2004). Are firm growth rates random? Analysing patterns and dependencies. *International Journal of Industrial Organization, 22*(1), 79–102.

Renzetti, M. (2001). Corporate Finance: Financial Control. In N. J. Smelser & P. B. Baltes (Eds.), *International Encyclopedia of the Social & Behavioral Sciences* (pp. 2792–2797). Pergamon. https://doi.org/10.1016/B0-08-043076-7/04268-6

Robbins, D. K., Pantuosco, L. J., & Parker, D. F. (2000). An Empirical Assessment of the Contribution of Small Business Employment to US State Economic Performance *Small Business Economics, 15*(4), 293–302.

Robbins, D. K., Pearce, J. A. (1992). Turnaround: Retrenchment and Recovery. *Strategic Management Journal, 13*, 287–309.

Rocca, M. L., Rocca, T. L., & Cariola, A. (2011). Capital Structure Decisions During a Firm's Life Cycle. *Small Business Economics, 37*, 107–130

Ross, J., & Lemkin, J. (2016). *The hard thing about hard things: Building a business when there are no easy answers.* Harper Business.

Ross, S. A. (1977). The determination of financial structure: The incentive-signalling approach. *The Bell Journal of Economics, 8*(1), 23–40.

Rubio-Misas, M., & Gómez, T. (2015). Cross-Frontier DEA Methodology to Evaluate the Relative Performance of Stock and Mutual Insurers: Comprehensive Analysis. In M. Al-Shammari & H. Masri (Eds.), *Multiple Criteria Decision Making in Finance, Insurance and Investment* (pp. 49–75). Springer International Publishing. https://doi.org/10.1007/978-3-319-21158-9_4

Salim, M., & Yadav, R. (2012). Capital structure and firm performance: Evidence from Malaysian listed companies. *Procedia – Social and Behavioral Sciences, 65*(3), 156–166.

Salonen, T. (2010). *Strategies, Structures, and Processes for Network and Resources Management*. Köln: EUL.

Saunders, M., Lewis, P., & Thornhill, A. (2016). *Research methods for business students* (7th ed.). Pearson Education.

Scheld, A. (2013). *Fundamental Beta: Ermittlung des systematischen Risikos bei nicht börsennotierten Unternehmen*. Wiesbaden: Springer Gabler.

Schmalen, C., Kunert, M., & Weindlmaier, H. (2006). Erfolgsfaktorenforschung: Theoretische Grundlagen, methodische Vorgehensweise und Anwendungserfahrungen. In Institut für Agrarökonomie Universität Göttingen (Hrsg.), *Unternehmen im Agrarbereich vor neuen Herausforderungen: 45. Jahrestagung der Gesellschaft für Wirtschafts- und Sozialwissenschaften* (pp. 351–362). Göttingen: Gesellschaft für Wirtschafts- und Sozialwissenschaften.

Schmitt, R. (2009). The influence of the financial crisis on accounting regulations. *Accounting Horizons*, *23*(4), 491–507.

Schmuck, M. (2012). *Financial Distress and Corporate Turnaround. An Empirical Analysis of the Automotive Supplier Industry* (PhD Thesis). Munich, Technical University of Munich.

Schneider, H. (2010). *Determinanten der Kapitalstruktur*. Gabler.

Schueffel, P. (2016). Taming the beast: A scientific definition of fintech. *Journal of Innovation Management*, *4*(4), 32–54.

Schumpeter, J. A. (1934). *The Theory of Economic Development, Cambridge, Mass.: Harvard University Press* (Reprint 1997).

Schwenker, B., & Spremann, K. (2008). *Unternehmerisches Denken zwischen Strategie und Finanzen*. Wiesbaden: Springer.

Scott, J. H. (1977). Bankruptcy, secured debt, and optimal capital structure. *The Journal of Finance*, *32*(1), 1–19.

Scott, M. & Bruce, R. (1987). Five stages of growth in small business. *Long Range Planning, 20*(3), 45–52.

Securities Industry and Financial Markets Association [SIFMA]. (2022). *US fixed income securities statistics*. Retrieved from SIFMA.

Securities Industry and Financial Markets Association [SIFMA]. (2024a). *US corporate bonds statistics*. www.sifma.org/resources/research/us-corporate-bonds-statistics/

Securities Industry and Financial Markets Association [SIFMA]. (2024b). *US fixed income securities statistics*. Retrieved from US Bond Market Statistics. www.sifma.org/resources/research/us-fixed-income-securities-statistics/

Senderovitz M., Klyver K., & Steffens. P. (2015). Four years on: Are the gazelles still running? A longitudinal study of firm performance after a period of rapid growth. *International Small Business Journal Researching Entrepreneurship, 34*(4). https://doi.org/10.1177/0266242614567483

Senge, P. M. (1990). *The fifth discipline: The art and practice of the learning organization*. Doubleday.

Seward, J. K. (2016). *Non-Distressed Corporate Restructurings and Reorganizations: A Valuation Approach*. Cambridge: Academic Press.

Shanghai Stock Exchange (SSE). (2022). Annual IPO Statistics.

Shepherd, D. A., & Wiklund, J. (2009). Are we comparing apples with apples or apples with oranges? Appropriateness of knowledge accumulation across growth studies. *Entrepreneurship Theory and Practice, 33*(1), 105–123.

Shleifer, A., & Vishny, R. W. (1997). A survey of corporate governance. *Journal of Finance, 52*(2), 737–783.

Siegel, R., Siegel, E., & Macmillan, I. C. (1993). Characteristics distinguishing high-growth ventures. *Journal of Business Venturing, 8*(2), 169–180. https://doi.org/10.1016/0883-9026(93)90018-Z

Siemens. (2022). *Siemens sustainability report.* Siemens AG.

Siemens AG. (2022). *Siemens annual report.* Siemens AG.

Simerly, R. L., & Li, M. (2000). Environmental dynamism, capital structure, and performance: A theoretical integration and an empirical test. *Strategic Management Journal, 21*(1), 31–49.

Sirkin, R. M. (2006). *Statistics for the Social Sciences* (3rd ed.) Thousand Oaks: Sage.

Smith, M., & Graves, C. (2005). Corporate turnaround and financial distress. *Managerial Auditing Journal, 20*(3), 304–320.

Smithson, C. (2013). *Managing financial risk: A guide to derivative products, financial engineering, and value maximization.* McGraw-Hill.

Smolarski, J., & Kut, C. (2011). The impact of venture capital financing method on SME performance and internationalization. *International Entrepreneurship and Management Journal, 7*(1), 39–55. https://doi.org/10.1007/s11365-009-0128-1

Stehle, R., & Schmidt, M. H. (2015). *Returns on German Stocks 1954 to 2013* (SSRN Scholarly Paper ID 2497359). Social Science Research Network. https://doi.org/10.2139/ssrn.2497359

Stein, J. C. (1997). Internal capital markets and the competition for corporate resources. *The Journal of Finance, 52*(1), 111–133.

Stephan, A., & Fischer, E. O. (2008). *Betriebswirtschaftliche Optimierung. Eine Einfuhrung in die quantitative Betriebswirtschaftslehre.* Oldenbourg Verlag.

Stiglitz, J. E. (1969). A re-examination of the Modigliani-Miller theorem. *The American Economic Review, 59*(5), 784–793.

Stolowy, H., & Lebas, M. (2013). *Financial Accounting and Reporting: A Global Perspective.* Andover: Cengage.

Strebulaev, I. A. (2007). Do Tests of Capital Structure Theory Mean What They Say? *The Journal of Finance, 62*(4), 1747–1787. https://doi.org/10.1111/j.1540-6261.2007.01256.x

Sudarsanam, S., & Lai, J. (2001). Corporate financial distress and turnaround strategies: An empirical analysis. *British Journal of Management, 12*(3), 183–199.

Sunder, S., & Yamaji, H. (1999). *The Japanese style of business accounting.* Quorum.

Sustainability Accounting Standards Board. (2018). *SASB standards.* The IFRS Foundation.

Swaay, H. van, Leleux, B., & Megally, E. (2015). *Private equity 4.0: Reinventing value creation*. John Wiley & Sons.

Tabachnick, B. G., & Fidell, L. S. (2013). *Using multivariate statistics* (6th ed.). Pearson.

Taouab, O., & Issor, Z. (2019). Firm performance: Definition and measurement models. *European Scientific Journal, 15*(1), 93–106.

Tarek Al-Kayed, L., Zain, S. R. M., & Duasa, J. (2014). The relationship between capital structure and performance of Islamic banks. *Journal of Islamic Accounting and Business Research, 5*(2), 158–181. https://doi.org/10.1108/JIABR-04-2012-0024.

Tirole, J. (2005). *The theory of corporate finance*. Princeton University Press.

Tomczyk, D., Lee, J., & Winslow, E. (2013). Entrepreneurs' personal values compensation and high growth firm performance. *Journal of Small Business Management, 51*(1), 66–82.

Treyer, O. A. G. (2003). *Business Statistik*. Compendio.

Tsuruta, D. (2017). Variance of firm performance and leverage of small businesses. *Journal of Small Business Management, 55*(3), 404–429.

Vasiliou, D., & Daskalakis, N. (2009). Behavioral capital structure: Is the neoclassical paradigm threatened? Evidence from the field. *Journal of Behavioral Finance, 10*(1), 19–32.

Vătavu, S. (2015). The Impact of Capital Structure on Financial Performance in Romanian Listed Companies. *Procedia Economics and Finance, 32*, 1314–1322. https://doi.org/10.1016/S2212-5671(15)01508-7

Vernimmen, P. (2018). *Corporate finance: Theory and practice* (5th ed.). Wiley.

Vickers, I., & Lyon, F. (2014). Beyond green niches? Growth strategies of environmentally-motivated social enterprises. *International Small Business Journal, 32*(4), 449–470.

Vinnell, R., & Hamilton, R. T. (1999). A historical perspective on small firm development. *Entrepreneurship Theory and Practice, 23*(4), 5–18.

Volk, S. K. (2013). *Einfluss der Eigentümerstruktur auf Finanzierungs- und Investitionsentscheidungen in privaten und börsennotierten Unternehmen*. Technische Universität München.

Voon, J. P., Lin, C., & Ma Yiu, C. (2020). Managerial overconfidence and bank loan covenant usage. *International Journal of Finance & Economics, 27*(4), 4575–4598. Early View.

Wahlen, J. M., Baginski, S. P., & Bradshaw, M. T. (2016). *Financial reporting, financial statement analysis, and valuation: A strategic perspective* (8th ed.). Cengage Learning.

Wald, J. K. (1999). How firm characteristics affect capital structure: An international comparison. *Journal of Financial Research, 22*(2), 161–187.

Walker, P. (2017). *The Theory of the Firm: An overview of the economic mainstream*. Routledge. https://www.routledge.com/The-Theory-of-the-Firm-An-overview-of-the-economic-mainstream/Walker/p/book/9780367876791

Walker, P. (2018). *A Brief Prehistory of the Theory of the Firm*. Routledge. https://doi.org/10.4324/9781351041386
Wehrmann, C. D. (2018). *Exploring Internationalisation Effects on Firm Performance Quantitative Empirical Study among German, Swiss and Austrian Listed Companies* (PhD Thesis). Gloucester: University of Gloucestershire.
Wei, Z. (2019). *Machine learning applications in finance: Some case studies*. Imperial College London.
Weill, L. (2008). Leverage and Corporate Performance: Does Institutional Environment Matter? *Small Business Economics, 30*(3), 251–265. https://doi.org/10.1007/s11187-006-9045-7
Welch, I. (2011). Two Common Problems in Capital Structure Research: The Financial-Debt-To-Asset Ratio and Issuing Activity Versus Leverage Changes. *International Review of Finance, 11*(1), 1–17. https://doi.org/10.1111/j.1468-2443.2010.01125.x
Wenzelburger, G., Jäckle, S., & König, P. (2014). *Weiterführende statistische Methoden für Politikwissenschaftler: Eine anwendungsbezogene Einführung mit Stata*. Munich: Oldenbourg.
Wernerfelt, B. (1984). A resource-based view of the firm. *Strategic Management Journal, 5*(2), 171–180.
Wiese, H. (2021). *Advanced Microeconomics*. Springer Fachmedien Wiesbaden. https://doi.org/10.1007/978-3-658-34959-2
Wiklund, J., & Shepherd, D. (2003). Knowledge-based resources, entrepreneurial orientation, and the performance of small and medium-sized businesses. *Strategic Management Journal, 24*(13), 1307–1314.
Wohlenberg, H., & Plagge, J.-C. (2012). Capital Markets 2.0 – New Requirements for the Financial Manager? In U. Hommel, M. Fabich, E. Schellenberg, & L. Firnkorn (Eds.), *The Strategic CFO: Creating Value in a Dynamic Market Environment* (pp. 109–126). Springer. https://doi.org/10.1007/978-3-642-04349-9_7
Wooldridge, J. M. (2013). *Introductory econometrics: A modern approach* (5th ed.). South-Western Cengage Learning.
World Economic Forum. (2022). *The global financial and monetary system in 2030*. World Economic Forum – WEF.
Wu, W., & Au Yeung, C. (2012). The role of management style in capital structure decisions: Evidence from an emerging market. *International Journal of Finance & Economics, 17*(1), 23–38.
Yoon, E., & Jang, S. (2005). The Effect of Financial Leverage on Profitability and Risk of Restaurant Firms. *The Journal of Hospitality Financial Management, 13*(1), 35–47. https://doi.org/10.1080/10913211.2005.10653798
Zambon, S. (2013). Accounting and business economics: Insights from national traditions. In Y. Biondi & S. Zambon (Eds.), *Accounting and business economics: Insights from national traditions* (pp. XI–XXII). Routledge.
Zeitun, R., & Tian, G. G. (2014). *Capital Structure and Corporate Performance: Evidence from Jordan* (SSRN Scholarly Paper No. 2496174). https://doi.org/10.2139/ssrn.2496174

Ziebarth, G. (2013). *Wie finanzieren sich Unternehmen in Zeiten der Krise? Neue Antworten der Jahresabschlussanalyse*. Deutsche Bundesbank. https://docplayer.org/10784190-Wie-finanzieren-sich-unternehmen-in-zeiten-der-krise-neue-antworten-der-jahresabschlussanalyse.html

Zikmund, W. G., Babin, B. J., Carr, J. C., & Griffin, M. (2009). *Business research methods* (8th ed.). South-Western Cengage Learning.

Zimmermann, W. (2013). *Erfolgs- und Kostenrechnung*. Springer.

Index

For Product Safety Concerns and Information please contact our EU representative GPSR@taylorandfrancis.com
Taylor & Francis Verlag GmbH, Kaufingerstraße 24, 80331 München, Germany

www.ingramcontent.com/pod-product-compliance
Ingram Content Group UK Ltd.
Pitfield, Milton Keynes, MK11 3LW, UK
UKHW022109190926
475702UK00013B/1342
9781032899008